Healing the Rift With Your Adult Child

Finding Forgiveness and Building Resilience for a Promising Future

Laura Lamont

© **Copyright 2024 - All rights reserved.**

The content contained within this book may not be reproduced, duplicated or transmitted without direct written permission from the author or the publisher.

Under no circumstances will any blame or legal responsibility be held against the publisher, or author, for any damages, reparation, or monetary loss due to the information contained within this book, either directly or indirectly.

Legal Notice:

This book is copyright protected. It is only for personal use. You cannot amend, distribute, sell, use, quote or paraphrase any part, or the content within this book, without the consent of the author or publisher.

Disclaimer Notice:

Please note the information contained within this document is for educational and entertainment purposes only. All effort has been executed to present accurate, up to date, reliable, complete information. No warranties of any kind are declared or implied. Readers acknowledge that the author is not engaged in the rendering of legal, financial, medical or professional advice. The content within this book has been derived from various sources. Please consult a licensed professional before attempting any techniques outlined in this book.

By reading this document, the reader agrees that under no circumstances is the author responsible for any losses, direct or indirect, that are incurred as a result of the use of the information contained within this document, including, but not limited to, errors, omissions, or inaccuracies.

Table of Contents

INTRODUCTION 1

    LET'S TALK ABOUT FAMILY ESTRANGEMENT 2
        Real Stories of Estrangement 3
    WHY THIS BOOK? 4
    MY STORY AND WHY I WROTE THIS BOOK 5
        Is This Book Right for You? 6
    HOW TO USE THIS BOOK 6
    MOVING FORWARD 7

PART 1: UNDERSTANDING ESTRANGEMENT 9

CHAPTER 1: THE EMOTIONAL IMPACT OF FAMILY ESTRANGEMENT 11

    THE INITIAL SHOCK: WHEN YOUR WORLD TURNS UPSIDE DOWN 11
        The Physiology of Shock 12
    THE EMOTIONAL ROLLER COASTER: BUCKLE UP, IT'S GOING TO BE A BUMPY RIDE 13
        The Complexity of Mixed Emotions 14
    THE LONG HAUL: WHEN THE DUST SETTLES (BUT THE PAIN DOESN'T) 15
        The Impact on Identity and Self-Concept 16
    THE RIPPLE EFFECT: HOW ESTRANGEMENT IMPACTS OTHER RELATIONSHIPS 16
        Navigating New Relationships Post-Estrangement 17
    THE INVISIBLE WOUNDS: SHAME, STIGMA, AND ISOLATION 18
        Breaking the Silence: The Power of Sharing Your Story 19
    GRIEF AND LOSS: MOURNING WHAT WAS AND WHAT COULD HAVE BEEN 19
        The Complexity of Ambiguous Loss 20
    THE BODY KEEPS THE SCORE: PHYSICAL MANIFESTATIONS OF EMOTIONAL PAIN 21
        The Mind-Body Connection in Estrangement 22
    THE IMPACT ON SELF-ESTEEM AND IDENTITY 23
        Rebuilding Your Sense of Self 24
    THE CHALLENGE OF HOLIDAYS AND SPECIAL OCCASIONS 24
        Strategies for Coping With Holidays 25
    FINDING YOUR FOOTING: THE FIRST STEPS TOWARD HEALING 26
        The Power of Self-Compassion 27
    THE BULLET POINTS 28

CHAPTER 2: FAMILY DYNAMICS—THE ROLES WE PLAY 33

    THE FAMILY AS A SYSTEM: MORE THAN JUST A GROUP OF RELATED PEOPLE 33
    TYPECASTING IN FAMILIES: THE ROLES WE DIDN'T AUDITION FOR 34

THE CASTING CALL: HOW FAMILY ROLES GET ASSIGNED 35
THE CAST OF CHARACTERS: COMMON FAMILY ROLES 36
   The Hero *36*
   The Scapegoat *37*
   The Caretaker *38*
   The Lost Child *39*
   The Mascot *39*
THE IMPACT OF FAMILY ROLES ON PERSONAL DEVELOPMENT 40
BREAKING FREE: REWRITING YOUR ROLE 41
THE FAMILY SYSTEM'S RESPONSE TO CHANGE 43
HEALING THE FAMILY SYSTEM 44
THE ROLE OF FORGIVENESS IN FAMILY HEALING 45
THE ONGOING JOURNEY OF FAMILY DYNAMICS 46
THE BULLET POINTS 48

PART 2: SELF-REFLECTION 51

CHAPTER 3: THE JOURNEY TO SELF-AWARENESS AND REFLECTION 53

THE POWER OF SELF-AWARENESS: SHINING A LIGHT IN THE DARK CORNERS 53
   Practical Exercise: The Self-Awareness Check-In *54*
UNDERSTANDING THE ESTRANGEMENT: PIECING TOGETHER THE PUZZLE 55
   Practical Exercise: The Estrangement Timeline *56*
THE MOTHER-CHILD RELATIONSHIP: A CLOSER LOOK 57
   The Overexpressed Mother: Smothering With Love *57*
   The Underexpressed Mother: The Emotional Void *58*
   Practical Exercise: Mapping Your Mother-Child Relationship *59*
THE FATHER-CHILD RELATIONSHIP: ANOTHER PIECE OF THE PUZZLE 60
   The Absent Father: The Missing Piece *60*
   The Aggressive Father: The Intimidating Presence *61*
   The Impact on Family Dynamics *61*
   Practical Exercise: Reflecting on Paternal Influence *62*
EMOTIONAL AWARENESS: NAVIGATING THE SEA OF FEELINGS 62
   Practical Exercise: The Emotion Wheel *64*
BEHAVIORAL PATTERNS: BREAKING THE CYCLE 65
   Practical Exercise: The Behavior Log *66*
SELF-CONCEPT AND IDENTITY: REWRITING YOUR STORY 66
   Practical Exercise: The Values Clarification *67*
   Practical Exercise: The Self-Reflection Letter *68*
INTEGRATING YOUR INSIGHTS: MOVING FROM AWARENESS TO ACTION 69
THE RIPPLE EFFECT: HOW SELF-AWARENESS IMPACTS YOUR RELATIONSHIPS ...70
NAVIGATING SETBACKS: THE NON-LINEAR NATURE OF HEALING 71
LOOKING AHEAD: THE ONGOING JOURNEY OF SELF-DISCOVERY 72
THE BULLET POINTS 73

CHAPTER 4: SELF-COMPASSION—A JOURNEY TO HEALING 77

THE POWER OF SELF-COMPASSION 77
    The Three Components of Self-Compassion 78
BUILDING YOUR SUPPORT SQUAD 79
    Chosen Family and Friends 79
    Mentors and Role Models... 79
    The Power of Community 80
SELF-CARE: MORE THAN JUST BUBBLE BATHS 80
    Trusting in Life 80
    Physical Health: Your Body Is Your Ally 81
    Nutrition: Fueling Your Healing 81
    Sleep: The Ultimate Reset Button 82
    Mindfulness and Meditation: Calming the Storm Within 83
    Journaling: Your Personal Time Machine 83
    Writing Your Story: Becoming the Hero of Your Own Narrative 84
    Creative Outlets: Expressing the Inexpressible 84
SETTING BOUNDARIES: YOUR EMOTIONAL FORCEFIELD.................................... 85
    Establishing Limits 85
    Communicating Clearly.. 85
    The Art of Saying No 86
FORGIVENESS AND ACCEPTANCE: LETTING GO OF THE WEIGHT 86
    Self-Forgiveness: Being Your Own Best Friend.. 87
    Taming Your Inner Critic 87
    Forgiving Others: Releasing the Burden 87
    Acceptance: Embracing Reality 88
REDEFINING IDENTITY: BECOMING WHO YOU WERE MEANT TO BE................. 88
    Personal Growth: Turning Pain Into Power 89
    New Narratives: Rewriting Your Story 89
    Exploring New Roles and Identities 89
BUILDING RESILIENCE: BOUNCING BACK STRONGER 90
    Learning and Development: Feeding Your Mind 90
    Volunteering and Helping Others: Finding Purpose in Service.................. 90
    Developing a Growth Mindset... 91
PLANNING FOR THE FUTURE: CREATING YOUR OWN PATH 91
    Setting Goals: Charting Your Course... 92
    Visioning a Positive Future: Dreaming Big 92
    Creating New Traditions 92
EMBRACING IMPERFECTION: THE BEAUTY OF BEING HUMAN.......................... 93
    The Power of Vulnerability 93
    Celebrating Small Wins... 93
WRAPPING UP: YOUR HEALING JOURNEY 94
THE BULLET POINTS... 95

PART 3: THE ROAD TO RECONCILIATION 99

CHAPTER 5: REACHING OUT WITH HEART AND HOPE 101

Reflecting on Your Own Resilience 101
Signs of Emotional Readiness 101
Reviewing Your Personal Growth 102
Understanding Your Intentions 102

Choosing the Right Time 103
Assessing the Timing 103
The Virtue of Patience 104
Setting a Positive Tone 104

Crafting Your Message 105
Choosing Your Method 105
Writing With Empathy 105
Key Elements to Include 106

Respecting Boundaries 106
Understanding Their Boundaries 107
Setting Your Own Boundaries 107
Balancing Persistence and Patience 108

Effective Communication Strategies 108
Active Listening 108
Non-Defensive Language 109
Expressing Genuine Emotions 109

Apologizing Sincerely 110
Crafting a Genuine Apology 110
Addressing Specific Incidents 110
Avoiding Justifications 111

Offering to Rebuild the Relationship 111
Suggesting Next Steps 111
Being Open to Their Terms 112
Setting Realistic Expectations 112

Handling Their Response 113
Preparing for Different Outcomes 113
Managing Your Emotions 114
Being Patient 114

Maintaining Open Communication 115
Checking in Regularly 115
Encouraging Honest Dialogue 115
Showing Consistent Effort 116

Seeking Professional Support if Needed 116
Recognizing When to Seek Help 116
Exploring Family Therapy 117
Utilizing Support Groups 117

Conclusion: The Journey of Reconciliation 118
Recap of Key Points 118

Words of Encouragement *119*
Final Thoughts: Love, Patience, and Perseverance *119*
REAL-LIFE STORIES OF SUCCESSFUL RECONCILIATION... 120
Sarah and Mike's Story: The Power of a Sincere Apology........... *120*
The Johnson Family: Healing Through Family Therapy *121*
David and Emily: The Journey of Small Steps............................... *121*
APPENDICES 122
Sample Initial Outreach Letter.. *122*
Resource List *123*
Reflective Exercises... *124*
THE BULLET POINTS 124
KEY POINTS... 125

CHAPTER 6: HOW TO MOVE ON WITHOUT RECONCILIATION 129

THE POWER OF ACCEPTANCE.. 129
The Importance of Acceptance for Mental Health *129*
Differentiating Between Giving Up and Moving On *130*
Stories of Finding Peace Without Reconciliation *130*
CONTINUING SELF-CARE AND PERSONAL GROWTH 131
Pursuing Outlets and Social Connections Through Hobbies and Interests *131*
Making New Connections Through Support Groups.................... *132*
Continuing Daily Journaling and Personal Growth *132*
REDEFINING FAMILY RELATIONSHIPS 133
Building a Chosen Family.. *133*
Strengthening Other Personal Relationships................................ *134*
COMMUNITY INVOLVEMENT AND VOLUNTEERING 135
Finding Purpose Through Helping Others..................................... *135*
Turning Your Experience Into a Positive Force............................. *136*
MORE REAL LIFE STORIES: MOVING ON WITHOUT RECONCILIATION 136
Emily's Story: Finding New Purpose... *137*
Robert's Journey: Redefining Family... *137*
Sarah's Path: Turning Pain into Purpose *138*
STRATEGIES FOR CONTINUED HEALING 139
EMBRACING YOUR NEW CHAPTER 140
THE BULLET POINTS 141

CHAPTER 7: WRAPPING UP 145

FINDING PEACE IN YOUR NEW REALITY.. 145
THE POWER OF TRUSTING IN LIFE.. 146
INSIGHTS FROM OUR JOURNEY 146
Exploring Family Value Systems *146*
The Power of Empathy.. *147*
Breaking the Cycle of Blame and Resentment............................. *148*
The Impact of Early Attachment.. *148*

The Role of Self-Reflection and Understanding Family Dynamics 149
　Your Ongoing Journey 150

REFERENCES **153**

Introduction

If you're holding this book, chances are you're in the thick of one of life's toughest challenges: family estrangement. Maybe you're a mom who hasn't heard from your adult child in what feels like forever, or you're a brother or sister feeling like there's a Grand Canyon between you and your sibling. Perhaps you're dealing with radio silence from a parent, in-law, or another family member who used to be a big part of your daily life.

Whatever brought you here, I want you to know something right off the bat: You are not alone. The hurt, the confusion, the feeling of loss—it's all real, and it's all valid. Family estrangement is a deeply personal experience that often gets swept under the rug, but it affects millions worldwide. It's like a silent storm, leaving invisible scars and often wrapped up in a whole lot of shame and isolation.

I've been there, wading through the murky waters of family estrangement myself. I know about those nights when sleep won't come because your mind's too busy with questions and self-doubt. I understand that ache in your chest during holidays and family get-togethers. I've felt the struggle of trying to explain my situation to folks who just don't get it. And that tug-of-war between wanting to fix things and being scared of getting hurt again? I know that one, too.

I wrote this book to offer you a hand to hold onto—a source of hope and understanding in what can feel like a pretty dark and confusing time. *Healing The Rift With Your Adult Child: Finding Forgiveness and Building Resilience for a Promising Future* is here to walk alongside you on this difficult journey, offering insights, strategies, and, most importantly, a way forward.

Let's Talk About Family Estrangement

Before we go any further, let's get clear on what we mean by family estrangement. At its core, it's about physical and/or emotional distance between family members. It's when communication breaks down and relationships fall apart. This can happen between parents and adult kids, between siblings, or with extended family members.

The numbers tell us this is happening a lot more than we might think. A survey conducted by Karl Pillemer found that 27% of adults in the US said they were estranged from a family member (Pillemer, 2022). Over in the UK, a study by Stand Alone charity estimated about 1 in 5 families are dealing with this (Blake, 2015). That's millions of people grappling with this issue, often in silence.

Family estrangement isn't a one-size-fits-all issue. It can range from less frequent contact and emotional distance to a complete communication blackout. The dynamics can be all over the map—from a mother and daughter who've drifted apart to siblings who've stopped talking to in-laws who've cut ties. Each situation has its own story, its own set of feelings, and its own challenges.

Why does this happen? The reasons are as diverse as families themselves. Some common themes include:

- abuse—emotional, physical, or sexual
- neglect or feeling abandoned
- clashing values, beliefs, or ways of living
- old conflicts that never got resolved
- unhealthy family dynamics
- mental health issues or substance abuse
- divorce or remarriage

- arguments over inheritance

Often, it's not just one thing that leads to estrangement but a buildup of issues over time. It's important to remember that, for most people, cutting ties with family isn't a decision made lightly. It's often a last resort after years of trying to make things work.

Our society and culture play a part in this, too. We're living in a time where families are often spread out geographically. Many cultures are shifting toward valuing individual needs over family obligations. While great for connecting us in some ways, social media and technology can also highlight our differences and make conflicts worse. Plus, there's more awareness now about mental health and toxic relationships, leading some folks to prioritize their well-being over maintaining family ties that aren't healthy.

It's worth noting that estrangement can echo through generations. Patterns of distance and conflict can be passed down in families, creating cycles that are tough to break. Understanding this bigger picture can help us approach our situations with more empathy and insight.

Real Stories of Estrangement

To give you a sense of how varied family estrangement can be, let me share a few real-life stories (with names changed for privacy):

- Sarah, 42, hasn't spoken to her mom in five years. It started when Sarah came out as gay, and her mom, citing religious beliefs, couldn't accept her identity or her partner. They've tried to patch things up, but the hurt and disagreement are still there.

- Mark, 35, and his brother Tom, 38, stopped talking after a heated argument over their late father's estate. What began as a fight about money has turned into years of silence, with both brothers feeling betrayed and misunderstood.

- Elena, 29, made the tough call to cut ties with her dad because of his ongoing substance abuse issues. She loved him deeply but felt she needed to protect her own mental health and her young kids' well-being.

Like countless others, these stories show us just how complex and personal family estrangement can be. They remind us that there's no simple explanation or quick fix.

Why This Book?

You might be thinking, "How's this book going to help me?" Here's what you can expect to gain from these pages:

- **Understanding and Validation:** First and foremost, this book will help you see that you're not the only one going through this. We'll explore what family estrangement is, why it happens, and how it affects us, validating your experiences and feelings along the way.

- **Self-Reflection Tools:** You'll get some powerful tools to help you look inward, understand your part in the estrangement, and spot patterns in your family dynamics. This isn't about pointing fingers but about gaining clarity and insight.

- **Emotional Healing Strategies:** We'll dig into practical ways to handle the complicated emotions that come with estrangement—grief, anger, guilt, and more. You'll learn techniques for being kinder to yourself and building emotional resilience.

- **Communication Skills:** Whether you're hoping to reconnect or learning to set healthy boundaries, being able to communicate effectively is key. This book will equip you with skills to navigate challenging conversations and express your needs clearly.

- **Ways Forward:** Perhaps most importantly, this book will show you that you have options. We'll explore paths to reconciliation for those who want it and strategies for finding peace and moving forward if reconnecting isn't possible or something you want.

- **Personal Growth:** No matter what happens with your estranged family member, this book will guide you on a journey of personal growth and self-discovery. You'll learn to redefine who you are and find fulfillment beyond the pain of estrangement.

My Story and Why I Wrote This Book

You might be wondering why I'm the one writing this guide. As I mentioned earlier, I have personal experience with family estrangement. My family has a sad history of estrangement that affected an entire generation, leaving scars that we still feel today.

These experiences have given me a front-row seat to the complexities of family estrangement. They've taught me about the importance of protecting yourself and the possibility of finding peace even when relationships can't be saved.

Beyond my personal experiences, I bring professional expertise to this topic. Over the past four years, I've worked with many individuals struggling with family estrangement as a women's empowerment coach. I've guided clients through the process of avoiding family breakups due to issues like drug addiction, abuse, and neglect. My background as a business teacher has sharpened my communication and conflict-resolution skills, which are crucial when navigating family dynamics.

Moreover, my experience running businesses where I often employed individuals from challenging backgrounds—including ex-prisoners and young people from difficult family situations—has deepened my understanding of how family dynamics shape our lives and the potential for growth and change.

This book combines my personal journey, professional experience, and extensive research into family estrangement. I've written it with empathy, understanding, and a genuine desire to help others navigate this difficult terrain.

Is This Book Right for You?

If you're still on the fence about whether this book is for you, ask yourself:

- Are you struggling with the pain and confusion of family estrangement?

- Do you want to understand why this has happened and what you can do about it?

- Are you looking for ways to heal, whether getting back together is possible or not?

- Do you want to learn how to communicate more effectively with estranged family members?

- Are you ready to start a journey of self-discovery and personal growth?

If you nodded "yes" to any of these, this book is for you. Whether you're just starting to deal with family estrangement or have been grappling with it for years, whether you're hoping to reconnect or learning to move forward separately, this book offers valuable insights and practical strategies.

How to Use This Book

Healing the Rift With Your Adult Child is your compassionate guide through the complex journey of family estrangement. To get the most out of this book:

1. **First Read-Through:** We recommend reading the book from cover to cover initially. This will give you a comprehensive understanding of the estrangement process, coping strategies, and potential paths forward.

2. **Reflective Pause:** After your initial read, take some time to reflect on your personal situation and how the book's insights apply to you.

3. **Targeted Re-Reading:** As you navigate different stages of your estrangement journey, return to specific chapters that resonate with your current needs:

    - Struggling with emotions? Revisit the emotional healing strategies.

    - Considering reaching out? Review the communication skills section.

    - Unsure about reconciliation? Re-read the chapters on moving forward with or without reconnection.

4. **Ongoing Support:** Keep this book close as a source of comfort and guidance. Use it as a reference tool whenever you face new challenges or need a reminder of your growth and resilience.

Remember, healing is not linear. This book is designed to support you at every step, whether you're just starting to understand your estrangement or are well along in your healing journey.

Wishing you strength and peace as you navigate this path.

Moving Forward

As we start this journey together, I want you to know there's hope. While family estrangement is painful, it doesn't have to define your entire life. This book will guide you toward understanding, healing, and growth.

In the chapters ahead, we'll explore how estrangement affects us emotionally, examine family dynamics, and provide tools for self-reflection and healing. We'll discuss strategies for reaching out and rebuilding relationships and how to find peace if getting back together isn't possible. Throughout, we'll share real-life stories of people who've navigated family estrangement, offering both inspiration and practical insights.

Remember, this is your journey. There's no right or wrong way to handle family estrangement. This book is here to support you, offering guidance and tools, but ultimately, you'll choose the path that's right for you.

As we begin, I invite you to approach this book with an open heart and mind. Be gentle with yourself as you explore these challenging topics. And above all, hold onto hope. Whether your path leads to reconciliation or finding peace and fulfillment in a life redefined, know that healing is possible.

Part 1:

Understanding Estrangement

Family estrangement is a profound and often misunderstood experience that touches the lives of millions. It's a subject that many find difficult to discuss, shrouded in silence, shame, and societal expectations of what family relationships should look like. Yet, for those navigating the choppy waters of estrangement, understanding this complex phenomenon is the first crucial step toward healing and potential reconciliation.

Part 1 of this book begins a journey to demystify family estrangement. We'll peel back the layers of this painful experience, exploring its emotional landscape and the intricate family dynamics that often contribute to it. This section serves as a foundation, providing you with the knowledge and insights necessary to navigate your personal journey through estrangement.

Chapter 1 examines the emotional impact of estrangement. Here, we'll explore the roller coaster of feelings that often accompany this experience—from shock and disbelief to anger, guilt, and profound sadness. We'll discuss how estrangement can shake the very foundations of our identity and self-worth and how it ripples out to affect other relationships in our lives. By shining a light on these emotions, we aim to validate your experiences and help you understand that you're not alone in your feelings.

In Chapter 2, we'll take a closer look at family dynamics and the roles we play within our family systems. We'll explore how these roles are assigned, often unconsciously, and how they can contribute to patterns of conflict and estrangement. Understanding these dynamics can be a powerful tool for breaking free from destructive patterns and paving the way for healthier relationships.

Throughout these chapters, you'll find real-life stories from individuals who have walked this path before you. Their experiences, challenges, and insights offer both comfort and practical wisdom. You'll also encounter exercises designed to help you reflect on your situation, gain new perspectives, and begin the process of healing.

It's important to note that understanding estrangement isn't about assigning blame or finding simple solutions. Family relationships are complex, and estrangement rarely has a single, clear-cut cause. Instead, this section aims to provide a framework for making sense of your experiences and a starting point for your journey of healing and growth.

As we begin this exploration, remember that knowledge is power. By understanding the nature of estrangement, you equip yourself with the tools to navigate this challenging terrain. Whether you're a parent estranged from an adult child, an adult child estranged from a parent, or someone supporting a loved one through estrangement, this section will provide valuable insights to light your path forward.

Approach these chapters with an open mind and a compassionate heart—both for yourself and others involved in your estrangement story. Understanding is the first step toward healing, and you've already taken that crucial first step by opening this book. Let's begin this journey together toward greater understanding, healing, and hope.

Chapter 1:

The Emotional Impact of Family Estrangement

Let's talk about feelings for a minute—not just any feelings, but the kind that hit you like a ton of bricks when family relationships fall apart. If you're reading this, chances are you know exactly what I'm talking about. Family estrangement isn't just a fancy term for family drama; it's a profound experience that shakes us to our core and leaves us questioning everything we thought we knew about love, belonging, and identity.

In this chapter, we'll unpack the emotional baggage that comes with family estrangement. It's heavy stuff, I know. But here's the thing: Understanding these emotions is the first step toward healing. So, let's roll up our sleeves and dig in.

The Initial Shock: When Your World Turns Upside Down

Picture this: You're going about your day, maybe sipping your morning coffee or scrolling through your phone, when suddenly—boom!—something happens that changes everything. Maybe it's a heated argument that ends with someone storming out and not coming back, or perhaps it's a gradual realization that the distance between you and a family member has grown too wide to bridge.

Whatever the catalyst, that moment of realization is like an earthquake in your emotional landscape. Everything you thought was solid ground suddenly starts to shift. You might feel:

- **Shock:** "Is this really happening?"

- **Disbelief:** "This can't be real. It's just a bad dream, right?"

- **Confusion:** "How did we get here? What went wrong?"

Sarah, a 35-year-old teacher, describes the moment she realized her relationship with her mother had reached a breaking point: "It was like the floor dropped out from under me. One minute, we were having what I thought was a normal conversation, and the next, she was telling me she needed 'space' and didn't want to talk to me anymore. I felt like I was in a movie; it didn't seem real."

This initial shock can be paralyzing. You might find yourself replaying conversations in your head, searching for clues you might have missed. You might vacillate between wanting to fix things immediately and feeling completely overwhelmed by the situation.

It's important to remember that this shock is a normal response to an abnormal situation. Our brains are wired for connection, especially with family. When that connection is threatened or severed, it triggers our fight-or-flight response. You're not overreacting or being dramatic; you're having a very human response to a profound loss.

The Physiology of Shock

Understanding what's happening in your body during this initial shock can be helpful. When we experience a traumatic event—and yes, family estrangement can absolutely be traumatic—our bodies release a flood of stress hormones like cortisol and adrenaline. This can lead to physical symptoms such as:

- rapid heartbeat

- shortness of breath

- nausea or upset stomach

- dizziness or lightheadedness

- muscle tension or trembling

These physical reactions are your body's way of trying to protect you. It's gearing up to face a threat, even if that threat isn't something you can fight or flee from in a literal sense. Recognizing these symptoms for what they are—a normal stress response—can help you start to regain a sense of control.

The Emotional Roller Coaster: Buckle Up, It's Going to Be a Bumpy Ride

Once the initial shock wears off, you might find yourself on an emotional roller coaster that would put any theme park to shame. One minute you're angry, the next you're overwhelmed with sadness. You might experience:

- **Anger:** "How could they do this to me? Don't I matter to them?"

- **Sadness:** A deep, pervasive sense of loss and grief.

- **Guilt:** "Maybe this is all my fault. I should have done things differently."

- **Relief:** Yes, even relief can be part of the mix, especially if the relationship was toxic or abusive.

- **Anxiety:** Worrying about the future and how this will affect other relationships.

- **Shame:** Feeling like you've failed or that there must be something wrong with you.

These emotions don't come in any particular order, and they certainly don't follow a neat, linear path. You might wake up feeling determined to move on, only to be blindsided by grief while doing something as mundane as grocery shopping.

Mark, a 42-year-old accountant estranged from his brother, shares: "I'd be fine for days, even weeks. Then, I'd see a pair of brothers laughing together at a restaurant, and I'd be a mess for the rest of the day. It felt like I was on an emotional seesaw, never knowing which way I'd tip next."

This emotional turbulence is exhausting, and it's not uncommon to feel like you're going crazy. You're not. You're processing a significant loss, and that takes time. Be patient with yourself. Allow yourself to feel these emotions without judgment. They're all part of the healing process.

The Complexity of Mixed Emotions

One of the most challenging aspects of this emotional roller coaster is the way different feelings can coexist or rapidly alternate. You might feel angry at your estranged family member one moment and miss them terribly the next. This emotional whiplash can be disorienting and distressing.

Lisa, a 50-year-old nurse estranged from her daughter, describes it this way: "There are days when I'm so angry I could scream. How could she cut me out of her life like this? But then, in the very next breath, I'm overwhelmed with worry. Is she okay? Is she taking care of herself? The back-and-forth is exhausting."

These conflicting emotions are a normal part of the estrangement experience. They reflect the complexity of family relationships and the depth of the loss you're experiencing. Acknowledging and accepting these mixed feelings, rather than trying to force yourself to feel one way or another, can be an essential step in processing your experience.

The Long Haul: When the Dust Settles (But the Pain Doesn't)

As time passes, you might expect things to get easier. And in some ways, they do. The initial shock wears off, and the intense ups and downs of the emotional rollercoaster start to level out. But that doesn't mean the pain goes away. Instead, it often transforms into a more chronic form of distress.

Long-term effects of family estrangement can include:

- persistent sadness or depression
- chronic anxiety
- low self-esteem and self-worth issues
- trust issues in other relationships
- difficulty forming or maintaining close relationships
- physical health problems related to chronic stress

Elena, a 29-year-old graphic designer estranged from her father, describes it this way: "It's like there's this constant low-level hum of sadness in the background of my life. Most days, I can ignore it, but it's always there. And sometimes, like during the holidays or when I see fathers and daughters together, it gets louder and harder to ignore."

One of estrangement's most insidious long-term effects is how it can erode your sense of self-worth. When a family member chooses to cut ties, it's easy to internalize that as a reflection of your value as a person. You might find yourself thinking, "If my own family doesn't want me, there must be something fundamentally wrong with me."

This kind of thinking can lead to a negative spiral, affecting your mental health and your ability to form and maintain other relationships.

It's crucial to recognize these thoughts for what they are: distortions based on pain, not facts about your worth.

The Impact on Identity and Self-Concept

Family plays a significant role in shaping our identity and self-concept. When estrangement occurs, it can feel like a fundamental part of who you are has been called into question. You might struggle with questions like:

- Who am I without this relationship?

- How do I define myself now that this key family connection is gone?

- What does this estrangement say about me as a person?

John, a 45-year-old marketing executive estranged from both his parents, shares: "For years, I defined myself as 'the good son.' I was the one who always did what was expected and who made my parents proud. When that relationship fell apart, I felt like I'd lost my identity. I had to figure out who I was outside of that role, and it was terrifying."

Rebuilding your sense of self after estrangement is a crucial part of the healing process. It's an opportunity to rediscover who you are and who you want to be, independent of family expectations or dynamics. While challenging, this process can ultimately lead to personal growth and a stronger, more authentic sense of self.

The Ripple Effect: How Estrangement Impacts Other Relationships

Family estrangement doesn't happen in a vacuum. Its effects ripple out, touching every aspect of your life, including other relationships. You might find that:

- You're hesitant to get close to others, fearing they'll leave, too.

- You overcompensate in other relationships, becoming clingy or overly accommodating.

- You struggle to trust others, always waiting for the other shoe to drop.

- You avoid forming deep connections altogether, preferring to keep things surface-level.

James, a 38-year-old software engineer estranged from his parents, shares: "After the estrangement, I found myself pushing away friends and even sabotaging romantic relationships. It was like I was trying to prove to myself that everyone would leave eventually, so why bother getting close?"

This impact on other relationships can be one of the most frustrating aspects of estrangement. You know, logically, that not everyone will hurt you the way your estranged family member did. But emotions aren't logical, and fear can be a powerful force.

Navigating New Relationships Post-Estrangement

Forming new relationships after experiencing family estrangement can feel like walking through a minefield. You might find yourself hyper-vigilant, always on the lookout for signs that someone might reject or abandon you.

Sarah, a 32-year-old teacher estranged from her mother, describes her experience: "When I started dating my now-husband, I was constantly waiting for him to realize I was 'too damaged' and leave. It took a lot of work to understand that not everyone in my life was going to treat me the way my mother did."

Learning to trust again after estrangement is a process. It requires patience, both with yourself and with others. It might involve:

- being honest about your experiences and fears with new people in your life

- setting healthy boundaries to protect yourself while still allowing for connection

- recognizing and challenging negative thought patterns about relationships

- seeking support from a therapist or counselor to work through trust issues

Remember, every healthy relationship you form is a step towards healing and a testament to your resilience.

The Invisible Wounds: Shame, Stigma, and Isolation

One of the cruelest aspects of family estrangement is how invisible it can feel. Unlike other forms of loss, there's often no public acknowledgment, sympathy cards, or casseroles left on your doorstep. Instead, estrangement often comes with a hefty side of shame and stigma.

You might find yourself:

- lying about your family situation to avoid awkward questions

- feeling like you don't fit in during holidays or family-oriented events

- isolating yourself to avoid having to explain your situation

- internalizing societal messages about the importance of family, making you feel like a failure

Lisa, a 45-year-old nurse estranged from her mother, describes it this way: "When my husband died, everyone rallied around me. But when I stopped talking to my mom, it was like this big secret I had to carry alone. People don't know what to say, so they don't say anything. And that silence feels so heavy sometimes."

The shame and stigma surrounding estrangement can be paralyzing. It's important to remember that you're not alone, even when it feels that way. Millions of people are going through similar experiences, even if they're not discussing it openly.

Breaking the Silence: The Power of Sharing Your Story

One of the most potent antidotes to shame is speaking your truth. When we share our stories, we lighten our burden and create space for others to do the same.

Michael, a 55-year-old teacher estranged from his son, shares his experience: "For years, I didn't tell anyone about the estrangement. I was so ashamed. But I took a risk one day and opened up to a colleague. To my surprise, he shared that he was going through something similar with his daughter. That conversation was a turning point for me. I realized I wasn't alone and that sharing my story could actually help others."

While it's not always safe or appropriate to share your experience with everyone, finding even one trusted person to confide in can make a world of difference. This might be a close friend, a therapist, or a support group for people dealing with family estrangement.

Grief and Loss: Mourning What Was and What Could Have Been

At its core, family estrangement is a form of loss. But it's a complicated loss—one that's often not recognized or validated by others. You're not just grieving the relationship as it was but also the idea of what that relationship could or should have been.

This grief can manifest in many ways:

- sadness over missed milestones and shared experiences
- anger at the loss of family traditions or connections
- regret over things said or left unsaid
- mourning the loss of the family you thought you had or hoped to have

David, a 50-year-old teacher estranged from his daughter, shares: "The hardest part is the milestones. Her college graduation, her wedding—I wasn't there for any of it. And it's not just the big moments; it's the everyday stuff, too. I'll never know her favorite coffee order or what makes her laugh. It's like grieving a person who's still alive."

This type of grief, often called "ambiguous loss," can be particularly challenging because there's no closure. Unlike death, where there's a finality to the loss, estrangement can feel open-ended. There's always the possibility of reconciliation, which can make it hard to fully process the grief and move forward.

The Complexity of Ambiguous Loss

Ambiguous loss, a term coined by family therapist Pauline Boss, refers to a loss that's unclear or lacks resolution. It's particularly relevant to family estrangement because the estranged family member is physically absent but psychologically present.

This type of loss can be especially difficult to process because:

- **There's No Clear Endpoint:** Unlike with death, there's always the possibility of reconciliation, which can make it hard to fully grieve and move on.

- **It Lacks Social Recognition:** Society doesn't have clear rituals or acknowledgments for estrangement the way it does for other losses.

- **It Can Lead to Frozen Grief:** The uncertainty of the situation can leave people stuck, unable to fully grieve or move forward.

Maria, a 40-year-old accountant estranged from her sister, describes it this way: "Some days, I feel like I've accepted the estrangement, and I'm ready to move on. But then I'll get a glimmer of hope—maybe she'll reach out on my birthday this year—and I'm right back at square one. It's exhausting, never knowing if I should be grieving or hoping."

Recognizing your experience as a form of ambiguous loss can be validating and can help guide your healing process. It acknowledges the unique challenges of estrangement and the ongoing nature of the grief you might be experiencing.

The Body Keeps the Score: Physical Manifestations of Emotional Pain

It's easy to think of the impact of estrangement as purely emotional, but the truth is that our bodies and minds are intrinsically connected. The stress and emotional turmoil of estrangement can manifest in physical symptoms, including:

- sleep disturbances (insomnia or oversleeping)
- changes in appetite
- headaches or migraines
- digestive issues
- fatigue

- muscle tension and pain

Maria, a 40-year-old marketing executive estranged from her siblings, recalls: "For months after the estrangement, I had these awful stomach aches. I went to doctor after doctor, but they couldn't find anything physically wrong. It wasn't until I started therapy that I realized how much the stress was affecting my body."

These physical symptoms are your body's way of processing and expressing the emotional pain you're experiencing. They're a reminder that healing from estrangement isn't just about addressing your thoughts and feelings; it's about taking care of your whole self, body and mind.

The Mind-Body Connection in Estrangement

The connection between emotional stress and physical health is well-established in scientific research (Salleh, 2018). Chronic stress, like that experienced during estrangement, can have significant impacts on your physical health:

- **Immune System:** Chronic stress can weaken your immune system, making you more susceptible to illnesses.

- **Cardiovascular Health:** Stress can contribute to high blood pressure and increased risk of heart disease.

- **Digestive System:** Stress can exacerbate conditions like irritable bowel syndrome (IBS) or acid reflux.

- **Chronic Pain:** Emotional stress can amplify feelings of pain or contribute to conditions like fibromyalgia.

Understanding this connection is crucial because it highlights the importance of holistic self-care during the estrangement process. Taking care of your physical health—through proper nutrition, exercise, and sleep—isn't just about feeling better physically. It's an integral part of your emotional healing process.

John, a 50-year-old business owner estranged from his parents, shares: "I started running after the estrangement, mostly to get out of my head. But I found that on days when I ran, I was better able to handle the emotional ups and downs. It was like the physical activity was helping me process the emotional stuff."

Remember, acknowledging these physical symptoms isn't about adding one more thing to worry about. It's about recognizing the deep connection between your emotional and physical well-being and using that knowledge to support your healing process.

The Impact on Self-Esteem and Identity

Family estrangement doesn't just affect our relationships with others; it can shake the very foundation of how we see ourselves. Our families often play a crucial role in shaping our identity and self-esteem. When that relationship is severed, it can leave us questioning our worth and who we are at our core.

You might find yourself grappling with thoughts like:

- "If my own family doesn't want me, who will?"

- "Maybe I don't deserve love or belonging."

- "I must be fundamentally flawed for this to have happened."

These thoughts can be incredibly damaging to your self-esteem and impact every aspect of your life.

Sarah, a 38-year-old teacher estranged from her parents, describes her experience: "For years after the estrangement, I felt like I was walking around with a big sign on my forehead that said 'Unlovable.' It affected everything—my work, my friendships, my romantic relationships. I was constantly trying to prove my worth, always afraid that people would 'find out' how unlovable I really was and leave me, too."

Rebuilding Your Sense of Self

Rebuilding your self-esteem after estrangement is a crucial part of the healing process. It involves:

- **Challenging Negative Self-Talk:** Recognize when you're being overly critical of yourself and practice reframing those thoughts.

- **Identifying Your Values:** What's important to you, independent of your family's expectations?

- **Setting and Achieving Personal Goals:** This can help you build confidence and a sense of self-efficacy.

- **Practicing Self-Compassion:** Treat yourself with the same kindness you'd offer a good friend going through a tough time.

- **Seeking Validation From Within:** While external validation feels good, learning to validate yourself is crucial for long-term self-esteem.

Remember, your family relationships do not determine your worth. You are inherently valuable and worthy of love and belonging, regardless of the status of your family relationships.

The Challenge of Holidays and Special Occasions

Holidays and special occasions can be particularly challenging when dealing with family estrangement. These times are often loaded with expectations of family togetherness, which can intensify feelings of loss and isolation.

You might find yourself:

- dreading the approach of holidays or family-centric events

- feeling a renewed sense of grief or anger during these times

- struggling with how to explain your situation to others

- feeling pressured to reconcile or "just get over it" for the sake of the holiday

Lisa, a 42-year-old nurse estranged from her sister, shares: "The first Christmas after the estrangement was the hardest. Everyone kept asking where my sister was, and I didn't know what to say. I ended up leaving the family gathering early because I couldn't handle the questions and the pitying looks."

Strategies for Coping With Holidays

Navigating holidays and special occasions during estrangement requires intentionality and self-care. Here are some strategies that others have found helpful:

- **Create New Traditions:** This can help shift your focus from what you've lost to what you're creating.

- **Surround Yourself With Supportive People:** Spend time with friends or chosen family who understand and support you.

- **Plan Ahead:** Having a plan for how you'll spend the day can help reduce anxiety.

- **Give Yourself Permission to Feel:** It's okay if holidays are hard. Allow yourself to acknowledge and feel your emotions.

- **Practice Self-Care:** This might mean taking time for yourself, engaging in activities you enjoy, or seeking extra support during these times.

Remember, there's no "right" way to handle holidays during estrangement. What matters is finding what works for you and being gentle with yourself in the process.

Finding Your Footing: The First Steps Toward Healing

If reading all of this has left you feeling a bit overwhelmed, take a deep breath. Yes, the emotional impact of family estrangement is profound and far-reaching. But here's the good news: Understanding these emotions is the first step toward healing.

By recognizing and naming these feelings, you're already starting to take back some control. You're shining a light on the dark corners of this experience, and in doing so, you're beginning to find your way forward.

As we move through the rest of this book, we'll explore strategies for coping with these emotions, rebuilding your sense of self, and creating a life of meaning and connection—with or without reconciliation. But for now, I want you to remember three things:

- Your feelings are valid—all of them, even the ones that don't make sense or that you think you "shouldn't" be feeling.

- You are not alone. Millions of people are on this same journey, even if it feels isolating right now.

- Healing is possible. It might not happen overnight, and the path might not be straight, but you have the strength within you to move through this and create a life of joy and connection.

The Power of Self-Compassion

As you begin this healing journey, one of the most powerful tools at your disposal is self-compassion. This means treating yourself with the same kindness and understanding you'd offer a good friend going through a tough time.

Self-compassion involves:

- **Mindfulness:** Acknowledge your pain without judgment or avoidance.

- **Common Humanity:** Recognize that suffering is a part of the human experience. You're not alone in your struggles.

- **Self-Kindness:** Treat yourself with care and understanding rather than harsh self-criticism.

Alex, a 55-year-old writer who's been estranged from his parents for over a decade, shares his experience with self-compassion: "The first few years were hell. I felt like I was walking around with this gaping wound that no one could see. But slowly, so slowly I barely noticed it at first, things started to shift. I learned to be kinder to myself. I stopped beating myself up for feeling sad or angry. I started to build a life that was truly mine. I found my chosen family. I learned to parent myself in the ways my parents never could. And while there's still sadness sometimes, it no longer defines me. If you're in the thick of it right now, hold on. It does get better."

Remember, acknowledging and understanding your emotions isn't about wallowing in pain; it's about creating a foundation for healing. In the next chapter, we'll start exploring tools and strategies to help you navigate these turbulent emotional waters and start building a path toward healing and growth.

You've taken the first step. You're here, you're reading, you're trying to understand. That takes courage. Hold onto that courage—you're going to need it for the journey ahead. But I promise you, it's a journey worth taking.

As we close this chapter, I want you to take a moment to acknowledge yourself. You're facing one of life's most challenging experiences head-on. You're seeking understanding and growth in the face of pain. That's no small thing. Be proud of yourself for that.

In the chapters to come, we'll build on this foundation of understanding. We'll explore practical strategies for coping, healing, and moving forward. But for now, simply recognizing and naming these emotions is enough. You're doing the work, and that's what matters.

Remember, healing isn't linear. There will be good days and bad days. But with each step forward, you're building resilience, strength, and a deeper understanding of yourself. And that, my friend, is something to be celebrated.

The Bullet Points

Let's take a moment to reflect on the key points we've covered. This summary is a road map of the complex emotional terrain we've explored together. Whether you're just beginning to navigate the choppy waters of estrangement or are further along in your journey, this overview can help you understand and validate your experiences. Use it as a reference point when you need a reminder that your feelings are normal or as a tool to explain your experience to others. Remember, recognizing these emotions is the first step toward healing.

- **Initial Shock**
    - It feels like an emotional earthquake.
    - It can trigger physical symptoms due to stress hormones.
    - It is a normal response to an abnormal situation.
- **Emotional Roller Coaster**

- You will experience a wide range of emotions: anger, sadness, guilt, relief, anxiety, or shame.
- Emotions don't follow a linear path.
- Mixed and conflicting emotions are common.

- **Long-Term Effects**
    - persistent sadness or depression
    - chronic anxiety
    - low self-esteem and self-worth issues
    - trust issues in other relationships
    - physical health problems related to chronic stress

- **Impact on Identity and Self-Concept**
    - It challenges one's sense of self.
    - It is also an opportunity for personal growth and self-discovery.

- **Ripple Effect on Other Relationships**
    - You may be hesitant to form close bonds.
    - You may have trust issues in new relationships.
    - There is potential for overcompensation or avoidance in relationships.

- **Shame, Stigma, and Isolation**
    - You may have feelings of not fitting in, especially during family-oriented events.
    - You may isolate to avoid explaining the situation.

- o It is important to share your story to combat shame.

- **Grief and Ambiguous Loss**

    - o You will mourn what was and what could have been.

    - o There is the complexity of grieving someone who is still alive.

    - o There is a lack of closure and social recognition for this type of loss.

- **Physical Manifestations of Emotional Pain**

    - o You may experience sleep disturbances, changes in appetite, headaches, or digestive issues.

    - o It is important to address both physical and emotional health.

- **Impact on Self-Esteem**

    - o You may question your worth and lovability.

    - o You must rebuild your sense of self, independent of family relationships

- **Challenges of Holidays and Special Occasions**

    - o There may be intensified feelings of loss and isolation.

    - o It is important to create new traditions and practice self-care.

- **First Steps Toward Healing**

    - o Recognize and validate all emotions.

    - o Understand that you're not alone.

    - o Practice self-compassion.

- Acknowledge that healing is possible, even if not linear.

Remember: Understanding these emotions is the first step toward healing. Your feelings are valid, you are not alone, and healing is possible.

Chapter 2:

Family Dynamics—The Roles We Play

Have you ever felt like you were stuck playing a part in a play you never auditioned for? Welcome to the world of family dynamics. In this chapter, we'll explore the fascinating, sometimes frustrating, and often unconscious ways that families assign roles to their members. It's like a casting call you didn't even know you were attending, but somehow, you ended up with a starring role.

The Family as a System: More Than Just a Group of Related People

Before we jump into the specific roles, let's take a step back and look at the big picture. Families aren't simply collections of individuals who happen to share DNA or a living space. They're complex systems with their own unwritten rules, expectations, and patterns of interaction.

Think of your family as a mobile hanging over a baby's crib. When you touch one piece, the whole thing moves and shifts. That's how family systems work: What affects one member affects everyone, even if it's not immediately obvious.

Sarah, a 42-year-old teacher, describes her realization about her family system: "I always thought my brother's 'rebel' behavior was just him being difficult. It wasn't until I started learning more that I realized his acting out was connected to my 'perfect daughter' role. We were like two sides of the same coin, each playing our part to keep the family balance, even though it wasn't healthy for either of us."

Understanding your family as a system can be a game-changer. It shifts the focus from "What's wrong with this person?" to "What's happening in our family that's creating these patterns?" This perspective can be incredibly freeing, especially if you've been carrying around guilt or shame about your role in family conflicts.

Typecasting in Families: The Roles We Didn't Audition For

Now, let's talk about typecasting. In the world of acting, typecasting is when an actor gets pigeonholed into playing the same kind of role over and over. In families, it's not much different. Family members often get "cast" into specific roles based on their personalities, birth order, gender, or sometimes just family needs.

These roles aren't assigned in any official way. There's no family meeting where everyone gets handed their part (wouldn't that be easier?). Instead, these roles develop over time and are shaped by family dynamics, individual personalities, and often, the unconscious needs of the family system.

The tricky thing about these roles is that they can become self-fulfilling prophecies. If you're always seen as "the responsible one," you might start to take on more and more responsibility, even when it's not good for you. If you're labeled as "the troublemaker," you might start to live up to that expectation, even if it doesn't truly reflect who you are.

Mark, a 35-year-old accountant, shares his experience: "Growing up, I was always 'the smart one.' At first, it felt good to be praised for my grades. But over time, it became a trap. I felt like I couldn't ever make a mistake or show weakness. It took me years to realize that my worth wasn't tied to my achievements or intelligence."

Recognizing these roles is the first step in breaking free from them. It's about understanding that you're more than the part you've been playing in your family's story.

The Casting Call: How Family Roles Get Assigned

So, how do we end up in these roles? It's not like we filled out a job application or went through an interview process. The assignment of family roles is a complex process influenced by many factors:

- **Parental Expectations:** Parents often have conscious or unconscious expectations for their children. These might be based on their own upbringing, unfulfilled dreams, or societal pressures.

- **Birth Order:** Whether you're the oldest, youngest, or middle child can influence the role you're given. Oldest children are often cast as responsible leaders, while the youngest might be seen as the baby of the family.

- **Gender Stereotypes:** Traditional gender roles can play a big part in role assignment. Girls might be expected to be nurturing and emotionally expressive, while boys might be pushed towards leadership or stoicism.

- **Family Needs:** Sometimes, roles are assigned based on what the family system needs to function. If one parent is absent or struggling, a child might be pushed into a caretaker role to fill the gap.

- **Individual Personalities:** A child's natural tendencies can influence their role. For example, a naturally empathetic child might be cast as the family peacemaker.

- **Cultural and Societal Influences:** Different cultures have different expectations for family roles, and these can shape how roles are assigned within individual families.

Lisa, a 40-year-old marketing executive, reflects on how her role was shaped: "As the oldest daughter in a traditional Asian family, I was automatically assigned the role of second mother. I was expected to help with household chores and look after my younger siblings. It wasn't until I moved away for college that I realized this wasn't a universal experience for all oldest daughters."

Understanding these factors can help you see how your role developed. It's not about blaming your parents or your culture—in most cases, this process happens unconsciously. However, recognizing these influences can be a powerful step in deciding whether your assigned role still fits who you are and who you want to be.

The Cast of Characters: Common Family Roles

Now, let's take a closer look at some of the common roles that pop up in family systems. As we go through these, remember that these are generalizations. Real people are complex and might fit into multiple categories or none at all. The goal here isn't to put yourself or your family members into boxes but to provide a framework for understanding family dynamics.

The Hero

The hero is often seen as the family's success story. They're typically high achievers, responsible, and driven. On the surface, this might seem like a great role to have. After all, who doesn't want to be seen as successful?

But being the hero comes with its own set of challenges. Heroes often feel immense pressure to maintain their perfect image. They might struggle with perfectionism, have difficulty asking for help, or feel like they're never doing enough.

James, a 45-year-old lawyer, describes his experience as the family hero: "I was always the 'golden child.' Straight A's, captain of the debate team, first in the family to go to college. But inside, I was falling apart. I felt like if I showed any weakness, I'd be letting everyone down. It took a near-burnout in my 30s to realize I needed to redefine success on my own terms."

If you're the hero:

- Remember that your worth isn't tied to your achievements.
- Practice asking for help and showing vulnerability.
- Give yourself permission to make mistakes and be imperfect.

The Scapegoat

On the flip side of the hero, we have the scapegoat. This is the family member who seems to always be in trouble and gets blamed when things go wrong. Scapegoats often act out or rebel, which can reinforce their negative role in the family.

Being the scapegoat is a heavy burden to bear. These individuals often struggle with low self-esteem and might internalize the negative messages they've received from their family. However, scapegoats also tend to be truth-tellers in the family, often pointing out problems that others are ignoring.

Maria, a 38-year-old artist, shares her journey as the family scapegoat: "For years, I believed I was the 'bad kid.' Every family problem somehow became my fault. It wasn't until I started talking to others from similar situations that I realized a lot of my 'acting out' was actually a response to family dysfunction. I was saying and doing the things no one else was willing to address."

If you're the scapegoat:

- Remember that you're not responsible for all family problems.

- Recognize your strength in speaking the truth even when it's difficult.

- Seek support outside the family to build a more positive self-image.

The Caretaker

The caretaker, sometimes called the nurturer, is the family member who takes care of everyone else's needs. They're often emotionally attuned, quick to offer support, and may take on parental responsibilities even if they're not a parent.

While being caring is a wonderful trait, caretakers often struggle with setting boundaries and taking care of their own needs. They might feel guilty for having their own wants and needs or feel overwhelmed by the emotional weight of the family.

Sarah, a 50-year-old nurse, reflects on her caretaker role: "I was always the one everyone came to with their problems. I felt proud that I could help but also exhausted. It took me years to realize that it's okay to say no sometimes, that I'm allowed to have needs, too."

If you're the caretaker:

- Practice setting boundaries and saying no.

- Prioritize self-care and your own needs.

- Remember that you're not responsible for everyone else's happiness.

The Lost Child

The lost child is often the quiet one in the family, the one who tries to minimize conflict by becoming almost invisible. They might withdraw into books, video games, or other solitary activities as a way of coping with family stress.

Lost children often struggle with feeling overlooked or unimportant. They might have difficulty expressing their needs or making decisions. However, they're often highly creative and self-reliant.

Tom, a 32-year-old writer, describes his experience as the lost child: "Growing up, I felt like a ghost in my own family. With all the drama between my parents and my older siblings, it seemed easier to just fade into the background. It's taken a lot of work to learn how to speak up and claim space for myself."

If you're the lost child:

- Practice expressing your needs and opinions, even if it feels uncomfortable.

- Recognize that your thoughts and feelings are valid and important.

- Seek out connections and relationships where you feel seen and heard.

The Mascot

The mascot uses humor to diffuse tension in the family. They're often seen as the clown or the life of the party. While their humor can be a valuable tool for managing stress, mascots often use it as a way to avoid dealing with deeper emotions.

Mascots might struggle with being taken seriously or dealing with their own pain. They might feel pressure to always be "on" or to make everything okay through humor.

Alex, a 40-year-old teacher, shares his journey as the family mascot: "I was always cracking jokes, even in the most serious situations. It was my way of trying to make everything okay. But inside, I was hurting, too. Learning to let myself feel and express sadness or anger has been a challenge, but it's also been incredibly freeing."

If you're the mascot:

- Give yourself permission to feel and express a full range of emotions.

- Remember that it's not your job to manage everyone else's feelings.

- Practice being serious and vulnerable when the situation calls for it.

The Impact of Family Roles on Personal Development

Now that we've explored these common roles, you might be wondering: "So what? Why does it matter if I was the hero or the scapegoat in my family?"

Here's the thing: The roles we play in our families don't just stay in our childhood homes. They shape how we see ourselves, how we interact with others, and even the choices we make in our adult lives.

Let's break down some of the ways these roles can impact us:

- **Self-Perception:** Our family roles often become intertwined with our sense of self. If you were the hero, you might tie your self-worth to achievement. If you were the scapegoat, you might struggle with feelings of inherent "badness."

- **Relationship Patterns:** We often recreate familiar dynamics in our adult relationships. A caretaker might be drawn to partners who need "fixing," while a lost child might struggle with assertiveness in relationships.

- **Career Choices:** Our family roles can influence our professional lives. Heroes might gravitate toward high-pressure, high-achievement careers, while mascots might choose professions where their humor is an asset.

- **Coping Mechanisms:** The strategies we used to navigate our family dynamics often become our go-to coping mechanisms in adult life. A lost child might withdraw when faced with conflict, while a mascot might use humor to deflect from serious issues.

- **Mental Health:** Rigid family roles can contribute to mental health challenges. Heroes and caretakers might struggle with anxiety and burnout, while scapegoats might battle with depression or substance abuse.

Lisa, a 45-year-old HR manager, shares how her role as the family hero impacted her adult life: "I carried that need to be perfect into my career and my marriage. I was constantly striving, never feeling good enough. It took a toll on my mental health and my relationships. Learning to let go of that perfectionism has been a journey, but it's made such a difference in my happiness and my connections with others."

Understanding how your family role has shaped you isn't about placing blame or making excuses. It's about gaining insight into your patterns and behaviors. This awareness is the first step toward making conscious choices about who you want to be and how you want to live—beyond the role you were assigned in your family.

Breaking Free: Rewriting Your Role

So, you've identified your family role and recognized how it's impacting your life. Now what? The good news is that you're not stuck in your assigned role forever. You have the power to rewrite your part in your own life story.

Here are some strategies for breaking free from limiting family roles:

- **Know That Awareness Is Key:** Simply recognizing your family role and how it affects you is a huge step. Pay attention to when you're slipping into old patterns.

- **Challenge Your Beliefs:** Question the beliefs that come with your role. Are they really true? Do they serve you in your adult life?

- **Expand Your Range:** Experiment with behaviors outside your typical role. If you're a Caretaker, practice saying no. If you're a Lost Child, try speaking up more.

- **Set Boundaries:** Learn to set healthy boundaries, both with your family of origin and in your current relationships.

- **Seek Support:** Consider therapy or support groups to help you work through ingrained patterns. Sometimes, an outside perspective can be invaluable.

- **Practice Self-Compassion:** Be patient and kind with yourself as you navigate this change. Breaking long-standing patterns takes time.

- **Redefine Your Identity:** Actively work on defining who you are outside of your family role. What are your values, passions, and goals?

Mark, a 50-year-old former scapegoat, shares his journey of breaking free: "For years, I acted out the 'black sheep' role, even in my workplace and friendships. Attending a support group helped me realize that I had a choice. I didn't have to be the troublemaker anymore. Learning to see myself differently and to behave in ways that aligned with who I really am was hard work, but it's transformed my life."

Remember, change doesn't happen overnight. You might find yourself slipping back into old roles, especially when you're with your family or under stress. That's okay. Each time you notice it happening is an opportunity to make a different choice.

The Family System's Response to Change

Here's something important to keep in mind as you work on changing your role: Your family might not like it. Remember that mobile we talked about at the beginning of the chapter? When you start to change your part, it affects the whole system.

You might encounter resistance from family members as you try to break free from your assigned role. They might try to pull you back into familiar patterns or express discomfort with your new behaviors. This doesn't mean they don't love you or want you to grow. It's just that change, even positive change, can be uncomfortable for systems that are used to operating in a certain way.

Sarah, a 40-year-old former lost child, describes her family's reaction to her changes: "When I started speaking up more and setting boundaries, my family didn't know how to handle it. My mom would say things like, 'You've changed,' in a way that made it sound like a bad thing. It was tough, but I had to keep reminding myself that I was making healthy changes, even if it rocked the boat a bit."

As you work on redefining your role, it's important to:

- **Expect Some Pushback:** Understand that resistance is normal and doesn't mean you're doing anything wrong.

- **Stay Committed to Your Growth:** Remember why you're making these changes and stay true to your path.

- **Communicate Openly:** If possible, talk to your family about the changes you're making and why they're important to you.

- **Be Patient:** Give your family time to adjust to the new you. They might need time to recalibrate their expectations and behaviors.

- **Seek Support Outside the Family:** Having a support system that encourages your growth can be crucial during this transition.

Healing the Family System

While this chapter has focused a lot on individual roles and personal growth, it's worth noting that healing can happen on a family level, too. As you work on changing your role, you might find that it opens up opportunities for your whole family system to evolve.

This doesn't mean you're responsible for changing your entire family. That's not your job, and it's not even possible. However, your personal growth can sometimes be a catalyst for positive change in your family relationships.

Here are a few ways this might happen:

- **Opening Communication:** As you learn to express yourself more authentically, it might encourage other family members to do the same. This can lead to more honest, healthier interactions.

- **Breaking Dysfunctional Patterns:** When you refuse to play your assigned role, it can disrupt unhealthy family patterns, potentially leading to more balanced relationships.

Alex, a 48-year-old former hero, shares how his personal growth affected his family: "When I started setting boundaries and stopped trying to fix everything, it was rocky at first. But over time, something amazing happened. My sister, who had always been the 'problem child,' started stepping up more. It was like by stepping back, I gave her space to grow. Our relationship is so much better now."

Remember, family healing is a complex process that requires willingness and effort from all involved. You can't control how others respond, but you can control your actions and reactions.

The Role of Forgiveness in Family Healing

As you navigate these changes in your family role and dynamics, you might find yourself grappling with feelings of anger, hurt, or resentment. This is where forgiveness can play a crucial role—not for the sake of others, but for your own healing.

Now, let's be clear: Forgiveness doesn't mean excusing harmful behavior or pretending everything is fine. It's not about letting anyone off the hook or forcing reconciliation. Instead, forgiveness is about freeing yourself from the burden of anger and resentment.

Forgiveness can be especially challenging when it comes to family because the hurts often run deep, and the relationships are complex. But holding onto anger can keep you stuck in your old role and patterns.

Maria, a 55-year-old former scapegoat, describes her journey with forgiveness: "For years, I was so angry at my parents for always blaming me for everything. That anger kept me playing the rebel role well into adulthood. Learning to forgive was hard, but it allowed me to let go of that role and figure out who I really am."

Here are some steps you might consider in your forgiveness journey:

1. **Acknowledge the Hurt:** Before you can forgive, it's important to fully acknowledge what happened and how it affected you.

2. **Feel Your Feelings:** Allow yourself to feel angry, sad, or whatever emotions come up. These feelings are valid and part of the healing process.

3. **Shift Your Perspective:** Try to understand the larger family dynamics at play. This doesn't excuse hurtful behavior, but it can help you see the bigger picture.

4. **Practice Empathy:** Consider what might have led your family members to act the way they did. Again, this isn't about excusing behavior but about understanding.

5. **Let Go of Expectations:** Forgiveness doesn't mean the other person will change or that your relationship will be magically fixed.

6. **Choose Forgiveness for Yourself:** Remember that forgiveness is about your healing, not about the other person.

7. **Seek Support:** Forgiveness can be a challenging process. Don't hesitate to seek help from a therapist or support group.

The Ongoing Journey of Family Dynamics

As we wrap up this chapter, it's important to remember that understanding and navigating family dynamics is an ongoing process. It's not about reaching a perfect end state where everything is resolved and everyone plays an ideal role. Life is messier and more complex than that.

Instead, think of it as a journey of continual growth and understanding. There will be steps forward and steps back, moments of insight and moments of frustration, and that's okay.

The goal isn't to create a perfect family system or to completely erase the impact of your family role; it's about gaining awareness, finding more freedom to be yourself, and creating healthier patterns—both within your family and in your life as a whole.

Here are some final thoughts to keep in mind:

- **Be Patient With Yourself:** Changing long-standing patterns takes time. Be kind to yourself as you navigate this journey.

- **Stay Curious:** Maintain an attitude of curiosity about your family dynamics and your own behaviors. There's always more to learn.

- **Focus on Your Own Growth:** While it's natural to want your whole family to change, focus on what you can control: your own actions and reactions.

- **Celebrate Small Wins:** Notice and celebrate the small changes and moments of growth. They add up over time.

- **Keep Communication Open:** If possible, maintain open and honest communication with your family members as you all navigate these changes.

- **Seek Balance:** Strive for a balance between honoring your family connections and maintaining your individual identity.

- **Remember That You Have Choices:** You always have the power to choose how you respond to family dynamics, even if you can't control the dynamics themselves.

James, a 60-year-old who has been working on family issues for years, offers this perspective: "Understanding my family role was like putting on a pair of glasses for the first time. Suddenly, so much of my life came into focus. But it was just the beginning. I'm still learning, still growing, still figuring out how to be me within my family. It's a lifelong journey, but it's so worth it."

As you continue on your own journey of understanding your family dynamics, be proud of yourself for doing this work. It takes courage to look at these patterns and even more courage to try to change them. You're not just doing this for yourself but for all the relationships in your life and potentially for future generations of your family.

Remember, you are more than your family role. You are a complex, evolving individual with the power to shape your own story. Your family history is a part of you but doesn't define you. As you move forward, carry with you the strengths you've gained from your experiences, the lessons you've learned, and the wisdom you've acquired.

- **Modeling Healthy Behaviors:** Your journey of self-discovery and growth can inspire other family members to examine their own roles and behaviors.

- **Creating Space for Change:** As you change, you create space for others to change, too. Your new behaviors might allow other family members to step out of their rigid roles as well.

- **Fostering Understanding:** Your insights into family dynamics can lead to greater empathy and understanding among family members.

The Bullet Points

This chapter delves into the intricate world of family dynamics and the roles we play within our family systems. The summary below captures the key concepts and insights, providing you with a quick reference guide to understand how these dynamics shape our lives and relationships. Use this overview to reflect on your family role and as a starting point for personal growth and healing.

- **Family as a System**
    - Families function as interconnected systems.
    - Changes in one part affect the whole system.

- **Family Roles**
    - Roles often develop unconsciously over time.

- o Factors like birth order, gender, and family needs influence roles.
  - o They can become self-fulfilling prophecies.

- **Common Family Roles**
  - o The Hero: High achiever, often struggles with perfectionism
  - o The Scapegoat: Blamed for family problems, may act out
  - o The Caretaker: Nurtures others, often neglects own needs
  - o The Lost Child: Withdraws to avoid conflict, may feel invisible
  - o The Mascot: Uses humor to diffuse tension and may avoid serious issues

- **Impact on Personal Development**
  - o It shapes self-perception, relationship patterns, and career choices.
  - o It influences coping mechanisms and mental health.

- **Breaking Free from Roles**
  - o Awareness is the first step.
  - o Challenge beliefs and expand behavioral range.
  - o Set boundaries and seek support.

- **Family System's Response to Change**
  - o Expect resistance as the system adjusts.
  - o Patience and persistence are key.

- **Healing the Family System**
    - Individual growth can catalyze family-wide changes.
    - Strive for open communication and break dysfunctional patterns.

- **Role of Forgiveness**
    - Forgiveness is for personal healing, not excusing behavior.
    - It involves acknowledging hurt, feeling emotions, and shifting perspective.

- **Ongoing Journey**
    - Understanding family dynamics is a lifelong process.
    - Focus on personal growth and maintaining open communication.

Remember: You are more than your family role. This understanding is a powerful tool for personal growth and improving relationships both within and outside your family.

Part 2:

Self-Reflection

As we move into Part 2 of our exploration of family estrangement, we turn our gaze inward. Self-reflection is a powerful tool in the journey of healing and growth, especially when navigating the complex terrain of estranged relationships. This section invites you to pause, look within, and gain deeper insights into yourself and your role in the estrangement dynamic.

Chapter 3 focuses on self-awareness and its critical role in understanding and potentially healing estrangement. This chapter guides you through the process of examining your thoughts, emotions, and behaviors with honesty and compassion. We'll explore how your past experiences, including your relationship with your parents, have shaped your current reality. Through practical exercises and thoughtful prompts, you'll have the opportunity to uncover patterns, beliefs, and behaviors that may be contributing to the estrangement.

Chapter 4 builds on this foundation of self-awareness, guiding you through personal growth and healing. Here, we'll explore strategies for building resilience, practicing self-compassion, and nurturing your emotional well-being. This chapter provides practical tools for managing difficult emotions, setting healthy boundaries, and redefining your sense of self beyond the estranged relationship.

Throughout these chapters, you'll encounter stories from individuals who have walked this path of self-reflection. Their experiences offer both inspiration and practical insights, reminding you that you're not alone. You'll also find exercises designed to deepen your self-understanding and promote healing. These range from journaling prompts to visualization techniques, each carefully crafted to support your growth.

It's essential to approach this section with gentleness and patience. Self-reflection can sometimes bring up difficult emotions or uncomfortable truths. Remember, the goal isn't to judge or criticize yourself but to understand with compassion. Every insight gained is a step towards healing, no matter how small it may seem.

This process of self-reflection is not about assigning blame—either to yourself or others. Instead, it's about gaining clarity, fostering personal growth, and opening up new possibilities for your life. Whether reconciliation is possible or not, the work you do here will benefit you in all areas of your life.

As you engage with these chapters, keep in mind that self-reflection is an ongoing process. You may find yourself returning to these exercises and insights many times on your journey, each time discovering new layers of understanding about yourself and your relationships.

Remember, by turning inward and engaging in this process of self-reflection, you're taking a courageous step toward healing. You're choosing to grow, understand, and open yourself to new possibilities. This inner work is challenging, but it's also deeply rewarding.

As we begin this phase of our journey together, approach it with an open heart and a curious mind. Be kind to yourself as you explore your inner landscape. Celebrate your courage in facing these challenges, and trust in your capacity for growth and healing. The path of self-reflection you're about to walk is a powerful one, filled with potential for transformation and renewed hope.

Chapter 3:

The Journey to Self-Awareness and Reflection

Let's roll up our sleeves and dive into the heart of the matter. Because at the core of understanding family estrangement and finding a path forward is understanding yourself. It's time to turn the spotlight inward and embark on a journey of self-discovery that might just change everything.

The Power of Self-Awareness: Shining a Light in the Dark Corners

Self-awareness. It's one of those terms that gets thrown around a lot, right? But what does it really mean, especially in the context of family estrangement? Simply put, self-awareness is about getting to know yourself—your thoughts, your emotions, your behaviors, and yes, even those parts of yourself you might prefer to keep in the shadows.

Think of it like this: You're the star of your own movie, but for a long time, you've been so busy acting out your role that you haven't had an opportunity to watch the playback. Self-awareness is like hitting that pause button and really seeing yourself on screen for the first time.

Sarah, a 45-year-old teacher estranged from her mother, describes her experience with self-awareness: "It was like I'd been wearing someone else's glasses my whole life. When I finally took them off and really looked at myself, it was scary at first. But it was also the most liberating thing I've ever done."

So, how do we start this process of self-awareness? Here are a few steps to get you started:

- **Pause and Observe:** Take time each day to simply notice your thoughts and feelings without judgment. What's going on in your internal world?

- **Ask Why:** When you notice a strong emotion or reaction, ask yourself why. What's driving this feeling or behavior?

- **Look for Patterns:** Start noticing recurring themes in your thoughts, feelings, and behaviors. Are there situations that consistently trigger certain reactions?

- **Get Curious:** Approach yourself with curiosity rather than criticism. Instead of "Why am I so messed up?" try "I wonder why I react this way?"

- **Write It Down:** Keeping a journal can be an incredibly powerful tool for self-awareness. It allows you to track your thoughts and feelings over time and notice patterns you might otherwise miss.

Remember, self-awareness isn't about judging yourself. It's about understanding. And understanding is the first step towards change and healing.

Practical Exercise: The Self-Awareness Check-In

Let's put this into practice. Set aside 10 minutes each day for a week to do a self-awareness check-in. Find a quiet place where you won't be disturbed. Close your eyes and take a few deep breaths. Then, ask yourself these questions:

- How am I feeling right now? (Try to name specific emotions.)

- Where do I feel these emotions in my body?
- What thoughts are going through my mind?
- What triggered these thoughts and feelings?
- How are these thoughts and feelings influencing my behavior?

Write down your answers. At the end of the week, look back over your notes. Do you notice any patterns? Are there any recurring thoughts or feelings? This simple exercise can be a powerful first step in developing greater self-awareness.

Understanding the Estrangement: Piecing Together the Puzzle

Now, let's apply this self-awareness specifically to your experience of family estrangement. Understanding the reasons behind the estrangement is crucial, but it's not always straightforward. It's like trying to put together a puzzle where some pieces are missing and others don't seem to fit.

Start by reflecting on the events, behaviors, and patterns that led to the rift. This might involve recognizing specific conflicts, miscommunications, or unmet needs. But be prepared: This process can bring up some tough emotions.

Mark, a 50-year-old businessman estranged from his father, shares his experience: "When I first started digging into why my dad and I stopped talking, I wanted to blame it all on him. But as I kept reflecting, I realized there were times I could have communicated better or been more understanding. It was hard to admit, but it was also empowering because it meant I had some control over the situation."

As you reflect on the estrangement, consider these questions:

- What were the major events or turning points in your relationship?

- Were there ongoing patterns of behavior that contributed to the estrangement?

- Were there unmet needs or expectations on either side?

- How did communication break down?

- Were there external factors (like other family members or life circumstances) that played a role?

Remember, understanding the estrangement isn't about assigning blame. It's about gaining clarity so you can move forward with greater awareness.

Practical Exercise: The Estrangement Timeline

Create a timeline of your relationship with the estranged family member. Start from your earliest memories and work your way to the present. Mark significant events, both positive and negative. Include:

- major life events (births, deaths, moves, etc.)

- conflicts or disagreements

- moments of closeness or connection

- turning points in the relationship

- the point(s) where estrangement began

As you create this timeline, pay attention to your emotions. How do you feel as you recall these events? Are there patterns you can see more clearly now? This visual representation can help you gain a broader perspective on the relationship and the factors that led to estrangement.

The Mother-Child Relationship: A Closer Look

Now, let's zoom in on a specific aspect of family dynamics that often plays a crucial role in estrangement: the mother-child relationship. In my work as a coach, I've seen how variations in maternal behavior can profoundly impact family dynamics and individual well-being.

On one end of the spectrum, we have the overexpressed mother, often manifesting as overprotective or over-nurturing. On the other end, we have the underexpressed mother, emotionally absent or, in extreme cases, narcissistic. Both of these extremes can contribute to family estrangement in different ways.

The Overexpressed Mother: Smothering With Love

The over-expressed mother often comes from a place of love, but her behavior can feel suffocating to her children. She might be:

- overprotective, shielding her children from any potential harm or discomfort

- overly involved in her children's lives, struggling to respect boundaries

- excessively nurturing, potentially hindering her children's independence

Lisa, a 35-year-old graphic designer, shares her experience with an overexpressed mother: "My mom always wanted to know every detail of my life. She'd call multiple times a day, show up at my apartment unannounced, and try to solve all my problems for me. I know she meant well, but it felt like I couldn't breathe. When I tried to set boundaries, she'd act hurt, which made me feel guilty. Eventually, I felt like the only way to find myself was to cut off contact completely."

If you recognize this pattern in your relationship with your mother, remember:

- Your mother's behavior likely comes from a place of love, even if it doesn't feel helpful.

- It's okay to need space and to set boundaries.

- Your journey to independence is a natural and healthy part of growing up.

The Underexpressed Mother: The Emotional Void

On the other end of the spectrum, we have the under-expressed mother. This might manifest as:

- emotional absence, where the mother struggles to connect emotionally with her children

- narcissistic tendencies, where the mother's needs consistently come before the child's

- neglect, where the mother fails to meet the child's emotional or sometimes even physical needs

Tom, a 40-year-old teacher, reflects on his relationship with his underexpressed mother: "Growing up, I always felt like I was invisible to my mom. She was there physically, but emotionally, it was like I didn't exist. My accomplishments were ignored; my pain was dismissed. As an adult, I realized I was constantly seeking validation from others because I never got it from her. The estrangement happened gradually. There wasn't a big blow-up, we just... drifted apart because there was never a real connection to begin with."

If this resonates with your experience:

- Recognize that your emotional needs were and are valid.

- Understand that your mother's inability to meet those needs is not a reflection of your worth.

- It's okay to seek the emotional connection and validation you need from other sources.

Understanding these maternal patterns can provide valuable insight into your family dynamics and your own emotional landscape. But remember, while these patterns can explain behavior, they don't excuse harmful actions. Your feelings and your need for healthy relationships are valid, regardless of the reasons behind your mother's behavior.

Practical Exercise: Mapping Your Mother-Child Relationship

Take some time to reflect on your relationship with your mother. On a piece of paper, create two columns:

1. In the first column, list how your mother expressed (or didn't express) love and care.

2. In the second column, write down how each behavior made you feel.

For example:

1. Mom always insisted on driving me everywhere. → I felt suffocated and untrusted.

2. Mom never asked about my day. → I felt invisible and unimportant.

This exercise can help you identify patterns in your relationship and understand how they've affected you. It's not about blaming your mother but about recognizing the impact of her behavior on your emotional development and your current relationships.

The Father-Child Relationship: Another Piece of the Puzzle

While we've explored the mother-child relationship, it's equally important to consider the role of fathers in family dynamics. The father's presence (or absence) and behavior can significantly impact a child's development and contribute to family estrangement. Let's look at two common patterns: the absent father and the aggressive father.

The Absent Father: The Missing Piece

Absence can be physical, emotional, or both. An absent father might be:

- physically absent due to work, divorce, or abandonment

- emotionally distant, unable or unwilling to connect with his children

- present but disengaged, not actively involved in the child's life

James, a 40-year-old engineer, shares his experience: "My dad was always working. He provided for us financially, but he was never there for the important moments. I grew up not knowing how to connect with him or other men in my life. It's affected all my relationships."

If you've experienced an absent father:

- Recognize that his absence is not a reflection of your worth.

- Understand that you may need to seek male role models or mentorship elsewhere.

- Be aware of how this absence might affect your relationships and self-esteem.

The Aggressive Father: The Intimidating Presence

An aggressive father might display:

- verbal aggression, including yelling, harsh criticism, or belittling
- physical aggression or violence
- controlling behaviors and rigid expectations

Sarah, a 35-year-old teacher, reflects on her aggressive father: "Dad's temper ruled our house. We were always walking on eggshells, never knowing what would set him off. It's taken years of work to unlearn the fear and self-doubt that environment created."

If you've experienced an aggressive father:

- Acknowledge the impact this has had on you emotionally and psychologically.
- Understand that his behavior is not your fault.
- Be aware of how this might affect your own behavior in relationships or conflict situations.

The Impact on Family Dynamics

Both absent and aggressive fathers can contribute to family estrangement in various ways:

- creating an emotional void that children struggle to navigate
- setting up patterns of avoidance or confrontation in relationships
- contributing to feelings of abandonment, fear, or resentment that can lead to estrangement

Understanding these patterns can provide valuable insights into your family dynamics and your own emotional landscape. Remember, while these patterns can explain behavior, they don't excuse harmful actions. Your feelings and your need for healthy relationships are valid, regardless of the reasons behind your father's behavior.

Practical Exercise: Reflecting on Paternal Influence

Take some time to reflect on your relationship with your father. Consider:

- How would you describe your father's presence (or absence) in your life?

- How has this impacted your self-perception and relationships?

- Are there any patterns in your own behavior that might stem from your relationship with your father?

Write down your thoughts. This reflection can help you understand the influence of your father-child relationship on your current experiences and relationships.

Emotional Awareness: Navigating the Sea of Feelings

Now that we've delved into some specific family dynamics, let's turn our attention to your emotional world. Estrangement often comes with a tidal wave of emotions—some of which might seem contradictory or overwhelming.

You might be feeling:

- sadness over the loss of the relationship

- anger at the circumstances that led to the estrangement
- relief if the relationship was toxic or harmful
- guilt about your role in the estrangement or about feeling relieved
- confusion about how to move forward
- anxiety about the future of your family relationships

Here's the thing: All of these feelings are valid. *Every single one of them.* There's no "right" way to feel about estrangement.

Alex, a 38-year-old software engineer estranged from his parents, shares: "For a long time, I tried to tell myself I was fine, that I was better off without the drama. But underneath, I was a mess of contradictory feelings. I was angry and sad and relieved all at once. Learning to acknowledge and accept all these feelings was a game-changer for me."

So, how do we navigate this emotional roller coaster? Here are some steps:

1. **Name Your Emotions:** Simply putting a name to what you're feeling can help you process it. "I'm feeling angry right now" or "I'm experiencing sadness" can be powerful statements.

2. **Accept Your Feelings:** Resist the urge to judge your emotions. There's no "should" when it comes to feelings.

3. **Express Your Emotions:** Find healthy ways to express what you're feeling. This might be through talking with a friend, journaling, art, or physical activity.

4. **Seek Support:** Don't go through this alone. A therapist, support group, or trusted friend can provide valuable support as you navigate your emotions.

5. **Practice Self-Compassion:** Be kind to yourself. You're going through a tough experience, and it's okay to struggle sometimes.

Remember, emotional awareness isn't about changing how you feel. It's about understanding and accepting your emotions as valuable information about your experience.

Practical Exercise: The Emotion Wheel

The emotion wheel is a tool that can help you identify and name your emotions with greater precision. It starts with six basic emotions at the center (joy, sadness, fear, anger, surprise, and disgust) and expands outward to more nuanced emotions. Here's how you can use it:

1. Draw a large circle on a piece of paper.

2. Divide the circle into six sections, like a pie.

3. In each section, write one of the basic emotions: joy, sadness, fear, anger, surprise, and disgust.

4. Now, create an outer ring and divide it into more sections. In these sections, write more specific emotions that relate to the basic emotion in the inner section. For example, under "anger," you might write "frustrated," "annoyed," "resentful," etc.

5. You can create even more rings, getting more specific with each one.

Use this wheel daily for a week. Each day, identify where your emotions fall on the wheel. This practice can help you develop a more nuanced understanding of your emotional landscape.

Behavioral Patterns: Breaking the Cycle

As we continue our journey of self-awareness, it's time to shine a light on our behaviors. How we act and react, especially in times of stress or conflict, often follows patterns established long ago in our family of origin.

These patterns might include:

- withdrawing or shutting down when faced with conflict
- becoming aggressive or confrontational when feeling threatened
- people-pleasing to avoid disapproval
- using perfectionism as a way to earn love or approval
- relying on humor to deflect from serious issues

Maria, a 42-year-old account manager, recognized a pattern in her relationships: "I realized I had a habit of pushing people away whenever they got too close. It was exactly what my mom did to me growing up. Once I saw the pattern, I could start to change it."

Identifying your behavioral patterns involves:

- **Reflecting on Past Interactions:** Think about conflicts or significant interactions in your family. How did you typically respond?
- **Noticing Current Behaviors:** Pay attention to how you react in stressful situations now. Are there similarities to how you acted in your family?
- **Identifying Triggers:** What situations or behaviors from others tend to provoke strong reactions from you?

- **Exploring the Origins:** Can you trace these behaviors to your family dynamics? How might they have served you in the past?

- **Assessing Effectiveness:** Are these behaviors still serving you well in your current life?

Once you've identified your patterns, you can begin to make conscious choices about whether these behaviors still serve you. If they don't, you can begin developing new, healthier ways of interacting.

Practical Exercise: The Behavior Log

For the next week, keep a behavior log. Every time you have a significant interaction or encounter a stressful situation, write down:

- What happened?

- How did you react?

- What were you feeling?

- What were you thinking?

- Can you identify any triggers?

- How effective was your response?

At the end of the week, review your log. Do you see any patterns? Are there particular situations or emotions that tend to trigger certain behaviors? This awareness is the first step in changing patterns that no longer serve you.

Self-Concept and Identity: Rewriting Your Story

Family estrangement often forces us to grapple with fundamental questions about who we are. Our families play a significant role in shaping our self-concept and identity. When that relationship changes dramatically, it can feel like the ground beneath our feet has shifted.

Sarah, a 36-year-old marketing executive, describes her experience: "After the estrangement from my parents, I felt lost. So much of who I thought I was was tied up in being their daughter, in trying to make them proud. I had to figure out who I was without that role."

Exploring your self-identity might involve:

- **Questioning Beliefs:** What beliefs about yourself do you hold that came from your family? Are they still true?

- **Identifying Values:** What's truly important to you, independent of your family's expectations?

- **Exploring Interests:** What activities or topics excite you? Are there interests you neglected because they didn't fit your family's expectations?

- **Redefining Roles:** How do you want to show up in your relationships, work, and community?

- **Embracing Growth:** How have your experiences, including the estrangement, helped you grow or develop strengths?

Remember, redefining your identity is not about rejecting your past or your family. It's about integrating your experiences into a fuller, more authentic sense of self.

Practical Exercise: The Values Clarification

Understanding your core values can be a powerful way to reconnect with your authentic self. Here's an exercise to help:

1. Make a list of 20–30 values that resonate with you. (If you need inspiration, you can find lists of values online.)

2. Group similar values together.

3. From each group, choose the one value that feels most important to you.

4. Narrow your list down to 5–7 core values.

5. For each core value, write a brief statement about why it's important to you and how you want to express it in your life.

This exercise can help you clarify what's truly important to you, independent of family expectations or societal pressures.

Practical Exercise: The Self-Reflection Letter

Here's a powerful exercise to culminate your self-reflection journey in this chapter. Write a letter to yourself addressing these points:

- What have you learned about yourself through this self-awareness journey?

- What patterns or behaviors have you recognized that you'd like to change?

- What strengths have you discovered or rediscovered in yourself?

- How has your understanding of your family dynamics shifted?

- What do you want to remind yourself of as you continue this healing journey?

Seal this letter in an envelope and put a date on it—perhaps 3–6 months from now. When that date comes, open the letter and reflect on how far you've come.

Integrating Your Insights: Moving From Awareness to Action

Now that you've done the hard work of self-reflection, you might be wondering, "What's next?" Awareness is crucial, but it's just the first step. The real power comes when we use that awareness to make positive life changes.

Here are some ways to integrate your new insights:

- **Set Intention-Based Goals:** Set specific, achievable goals based on what you've learned about yourself. For example, if you've recognized a pattern of withdrawing when you feel hurt, you might set a goal to express your feelings more openly in one relationship this month.

- **Practice Mindfulness:** Mindfulness can help you stay connected to your insights and catch yourself when you're slipping into old patterns. Even a few minutes of mindful breathing each day can make a big difference.

- **Seek Support:** Consider sharing your insights with a trusted friend, family member, or therapist. Sometimes, saying things out loud can help solidify our understanding and commitment to change.

- **Create New Rituals:** Develop small daily or weekly rituals that reinforce your new self-awareness. This could be as simple as a daily check-in with yourself or a weekly journaling session.

- **Be Patient and Compassionate With Yourself:** Change doesn't happen overnight. There will be setbacks and challenges. Treat yourself with the same kindness and understanding you'd offer a good friend.

Remember, self-awareness is an ongoing process. As you continue to grow and change, you'll likely uncover new insights about yourself. Embrace this as a lifelong journey of self-discovery.

The Ripple Effect: How Self-Awareness Impacts Your Relationships

As you develop greater self-awareness, you might notice changes in your relationships—not just with your estranged family member but with others in your life. This is because as we understand ourselves better, we're able to show up more authentically in our relationships.

Emma, a 48-year-old teacher, shares her experience: "As I became more aware of my tendency to people-please, which I'd learned in my family, I started setting better boundaries in all my relationships. At first, some people were surprised, but over time, my relationships became more genuine and satisfying."

Here are some ways your growing self-awareness might impact your relationships:

- **Improved Communication:** Understanding your own emotions and triggers can help you communicate more clearly and effectively.

- **Healthier Boundaries:** As you become more aware of your needs and limits, you'll likely find it easier to set and maintain boundaries.

- **Increased Empathy:** Understanding your own experiences can help you relate more deeply to others' struggles.

- **Authentic Connections:** As you become more comfortable with yourself, you may find it easier to form genuine connections with others.

- **Conflict Resolution:** Greater self-awareness often leads to better conflict resolution skills, as you can better understand and articulate your own position.

Navigating Setbacks: The Non-Linear Nature of Healing

As you continue on this journey of self-awareness and healing, it's important to remember that progress isn't always linear. There will be good days and bad days, steps forward and steps back. This is completely normal and part of the process.

John, a 55-year-old business owner, describes his experience: "I thought once I'd figured out all this stuff about myself, everything would be smooth sailing. But then the holidays came around, and I found myself falling back into old patterns with my family. I felt like I'd failed. It took me a while to realize that setbacks are part of the journey, not a sign of failure."

Here are some things to keep in mind when facing setbacks:

- **Understand That Setbacks Are Normal:** They're not a sign of failure but a natural part of the change process.

- **Use Setbacks as Learning Opportunities:** When you slip into old patterns, take time to reflect on what triggered it. This can provide valuable insights.

- **Be Kind to Yourself:** Self-compassion is crucial. Treat yourself with the same kindness you'd offer a friend who's struggling.

- **Reaffirm Your Commitment:** Use setbacks as an opportunity to remind yourself why this journey is important to you.

- **Seek Support:** Don't hesitate to reach out for help when you're struggling. A therapist, coach, or support group can provide valuable perspective and encouragement.

Looking Ahead: The Ongoing Journey of Self-Discovery

As we wrap up this chapter on self-awareness and reflection, I want you to take a moment to acknowledge the work you're doing. This isn't easy stuff. Looking inward, especially when you're dealing with the pain of family estrangement, takes real courage.

Now, I have a task for you: Find a quiet place where you won't be disturbed. Take out a journal or a piece of paper. I want you to write down everything you've learned about yourself from this chapter.

- What patterns have you recognized?
- What emotions have you identified?
- What new understanding do you have about your family dynamics?
- What aspects of your identity are you questioning or redefining?

This writing isn't about anyone else; it's all about you. Keep yourself central in this exercise. This is the start of your healing journey.

As you write, remember that this process isn't about shame or blame. It's about understanding, growth, and moving forward. Every insight you gain is a step toward healing and creating the life and relationships you want.

I want to emphasize that self-awareness and self-reflection are lifelong practices. The insights you've gained here are just the beginning. As you grow and change, you'll uncover new layers of understanding about yourself and your relationships.

You're doing important work. It might not always feel like it, but each moment of reflection, each new understanding, is a victory. You're laying the foundation for profound personal growth and healthier relationships—with yourself and with others.

In the next chapter, we'll build on this foundation of self-awareness to explore practical strategies for healing and growth. But for now, be proud of yourself for showing up and for doing the hard work of looking inward. You're on your way to writing a new chapter in your life story—one where you're the author, fully aware and empowered to create the narrative you choose.

Remember, you're not alone on this journey. Many others have walked this path before you, and many are walking it alongside you right now. Your experiences are unique, but the journey of self-discovery and healing is a deeply human one that connects us all.

Take a deep breath. You've taken an important step today. Trust in the process, be patient with yourself, and keep moving forward. Your journey to healing and self-discovery has begun, and it holds incredible potential for growth, healing, and transformation.

The Bullet Points

This chapter examines the critical process of self-awareness and reflection in the context of family estrangement. It emphasizes the importance of understanding oneself as a fundamental step toward healing and personal growth. Use this summary as a guide to reflect on your journey and as a reminder of the key concepts and exercises introduced in this chapter.

- **The Power of Self-Awareness**

- o Self-awareness is understanding your thoughts, emotions, and behaviors.
- o It provides clarity and control over your reactions and choices.
- o Practice regular self-reflection and mindfulness exercises.

- **Understanding the Estrangement**
  - o Reflect on events, behaviors, and patterns leading to estrangement.
  - o Focus on understanding rather than blaming.
  - o Create an estrangement timeline for perspective.

- **Mother-Child Relationship Analysis**
  - o The overexpressed mother is overprotective and overly involved.
  - o The underexpressed mother is emotionally absent and potentially narcissistic.
  - o This relationship impacts emotional development and adult relationships.

- **Father-Child Relationship Examination**
  - o The absent father is physically or emotionally distant.
  - o The aggressive father is verbally or physically intimidating.
  - o This relationship influences self-esteem and relationship patterns.

- **Emotional Awareness**
  - o Recognize and accept a wide range of emotions related to estrangement.

- It is important to name and express emotions.
- Use an emotion wheel for more precise identification of feelings.

- **Behavioral Patterns**
  - Identify recurring behaviors, especially in stressful situations.
  - Trace patterns back to family dynamics.
  - Keep a behavior log to recognize triggers and responses.

- **Self-Concept and Identity**
  - Reassess self-identity post-estrangement.
  - Explore personal values independent of family expectations.
  - Use values clarification for authentic self-understanding.

- **Moving From Awareness to Action**
  - Set intention-based goals.
  - Develop new rituals to reinforce self-awareness.
  - Practice patience and self-compassion during the change process.

- **Impact on Relationships**
  - Increased self-awareness can improve communication and boundaries.
  - There is potential for more authentic connections and better conflict resolution.

- **Navigating Setbacks**

- o   Understand the non-linear nature of healing.

- o   View setbacks as learning opportunities.

- o   It is important to seek support during challenging times.

- **Ongoing Journey of Self-Discovery**

  - o   Recognize self-awareness as a lifelong practice.

  - o   Continue to reflect and focus on personal growth.

Remember: Self-awareness is the foundation for healing and personal growth. It's a continuous journey that requires patience, compassion, and commitment. Your insights and efforts are invaluable steps toward creating healthier relationships and a more authentic life.

Chapter 4:

Self-Compassion—A Journey to Healing

Before we consider the possibility of reconciliation, let's take a moment to focus on you.–yes, *you*. The truth is, before we can even think about mending bridges with others, we need to build a strong foundation within ourselves.

Think of this chapter as your personal growth boot camp. We're going to boost your resilience, pump up your self-esteem, and fortify your self-worth. Why? Because these are your strengths in navigating the rocky terrain of family estrangement.

The Power of Self-Compassion

Let's start with a concept that might feel a bit foreign at first: self-compassion. It's not just a buzzword; it's a lifeline. Self-compassion is about treating yourself with the same kindness and understanding you'd offer a dear friend going through a tough time.

Sarah, a 42-year-old teacher estranged from her parents, shares: "For years, I beat myself up over the estrangement. I was my own worst critic. Learning self-compassion was like giving myself permission to breathe again. It didn't fix everything, but it made the journey so much more bearable."

You've been through a lot. Family estrangement isn't a walk in the park. It's more like trudging through an emotional minefield. And you're still here, still moving forward. That deserves some recognition and, yes, compassion.

The Three Components of Self-Compassion

Dr. Kristin Neff, a pioneering researcher in self-compassion, identifies three key components (Neff, 2024):

- **Self-Kindness:** Being gentle and understanding with yourself rather than harshly critical.

- **Common Humanity:** Recognizing that suffering and personal inadequacy are part of the shared human experience—you're not alone.

- **Mindfulness:** Observing your negative thoughts and emotions with openness and clarity without trying to suppress or deny them.

Try this self-compassion break when you're feeling stressed:

1. **Acknowledge Your Suffering:** "This is a moment of difficulty."

2. **Remind Yourself of Common Humanity:** "Difficulty is a part of life. Other people feel this way, too."

3. **Offer Yourself Kindness:** Place your hands over your heart and say, "May I be kind to myself in this moment."

Remember, self-compassion isn't self-pity or self-indulgence; it's about nurturing yourself so you can better face life's challenges.

Building Your Support Squad

Now, let's talk about your support network. You know the saying, "It takes a village"? Well, it's not just for raising kids. It's for raising resilient, whole adults, too.

Chosen Family and Friends

Your chosen family—those folks who stick by you through thick and thin—they're gold. Cultivate these relationships like your emotional well-being depends on it (because, in many ways, it does).

Mark, a 38-year-old accountant, found solace in his chosen family: "When I stopped talking to my dad, I felt so alone. But my friends stepped up in ways I never expected. They became my family. They celebrated holidays with me and supported me through tough times. They showed me that family isn't just about blood."

Action Step: Make a list of your ride-or-die support crew. Who are the people who lift you up, who see you for who you really are? Commit to nurturing these relationships.

Mentors and Role Models

Having someone who's walked a similar path can be incredibly powerful. They can offer guidance, hope, and practical advice that comes from lived experience.

Lisa, a 45-year-old entrepreneur, found strength in a mentor: "I joined a support group for people dealing with family estrangement. There, I met Janet, who had been estranged from her family for 20 years. Seeing how she had built a fulfilling life gave me hope. She became a mentor and a beacon of what was possible."

Action Step: Look for mentors or role models. This could be through support groups, books, or even public figures who have dealt with family estrangement. Their stories can be a source of inspiration and practical wisdom.

The Power of Community

While individual relationships are crucial, there's also immense power in being part of a supportive community. This could be a support group, a spiritual community, or any group of people united by a common interest or experience.

Jake, a 50-year-old teacher, found healing in community: "Joining a men's group changed everything for me. It wasn't even specifically about estrangement, but being in a space where men supported each other emotionally... it filled a void I didn't even know I had. It gave me a sense of belonging I'd been missing since the estrangement."

Action Step: Explore communities that align with your interests or experiences. This could be an estrangement support group, a hobby club, or a volunteer organization. The key is finding a place where you feel a sense of belonging and shared purpose.

Self-Care: More Than Just Bubble Baths

Self-care has become a bit of a buzzword, often reduced to face masks and spa days. Don't get me wrong, those things are great. But real self-care goes deeper. It's about nurturing your whole self: body, mind, and spirit.

Trusting in Life

This might sound a bit woo-woo, but stay with me. Learning to trust in life–to believe that you can handle whatever comes your way–is a game-changer. It's about embracing each moment with openness and resilience.

John, a 50-year-old artist, shares his experience: "After the estrangement, I was always waiting for the other shoe to drop. But slowly, I learned to trust in life again. To believe that I could handle whatever came my way. It didn't happen overnight, but that trust became my anchor."

Action Step: Start each day with a simple affirmation: "I trust in my ability to navigate life's challenges." Say it out loud, write it down, make it your mantra.

Physical Health: Your Body Is Your Ally

Taking care of your physical health isn't just about looking good (though that can be a nice side effect). It's about feeling good, having energy, and building resilience from the inside out.

Emma, a 35-year-old nurse, found strength in physical activity: "Running became my therapy. When I laced up my shoes and hit the pavement, I could process my emotions in a way I couldn't just sitting and thinking. Plus, the endorphins didn't hurt!"

Action Step: Find a physical activity you enjoy. It doesn't have to be running marathons. Maybe it's dancing in your living room, walking in nature, or trying out yoga. The key is consistency and enjoyment.

Nutrition: Fueling Your Healing

What we eat affects our physical health, as well as our mental and emotional well-being. Eating a balanced, nutritious diet can support your body and mind during the healing process.

Michael, a 40-year-old chef, found healing through cooking: "After the estrangement from my parents, I lost my appetite. Food was always a big part of our family life. But then I started exploring new cuisines, focusing on nourishing, colorful foods. It became a way to care for myself and reconnect with joy. Each meal became an act of self-love."

Action Step: Pay attention to how different foods make you feel. Try incorporating more whole foods, fruits, and vegetables into your diet. Consider keeping a food and mood journal to track how your diet affects your emotional state.

Sleep: The Ultimate Reset Button

Never underestimate the power of a good night's sleep. Quality sleep can improve mood, boost cognitive function, and increase resilience to stress.

Lana, a 38-year-old marketing executive, prioritized sleep in her healing journey: "I used to wear my insomnia like a badge of honor. But when I started prioritizing sleep—setting a consistent bedtime, creating a relaxing bedtime routine—everything changed. I had more energy to deal with my emotions, more patience with myself and others."

Action Step: Establish a consistent sleep routine. Improve your sleep quality and overall well-being by following these steps:

Maintain a consistent sleep schedule:

- Go to bed and wake up at the same time each day, even on weekends. This helps regulate your body's internal clock.

Create a relaxing bedtime ritual:

- Choose calming activities like reading a book, doing gentle stretches, or practicing meditation.

- Stick to your chosen ritual consistently to signal your body it's time to sleep.

Practice nightly gratitude:

- Before sleep, reflect on things you're grateful for. This promotes a positive mindset as you fall asleep.

The positive effects can carry over into the next morning, setting a good tone for your day. Every night before I go to sleep, I do my daily gratitude. It sends me to sleep in a positive mindset, which spills into the start of my day when I wake up.

Following these steps can improve your sleep quality and start each day with a more positive outlook.

Mindfulness and Meditation: Calming the Storm Within

When dealing with family estrangement, your mind can feel like a storm of thoughts and emotions. Mindfulness and meditation can be your umbrella in that storm.

Tom, a 40-year-old teacher, found peace through meditation: "At first, I thought meditation wasn't for me. My mind was too busy, too loud. But I stuck with it, just five minutes a day. Now, it's my daily reset button. It helps me stay grounded when memories or emotions threaten to overwhelm me."

Action Step: Start with just five minutes of mindfulness a day. Focus on your breath, or try a guided meditation app. Remember, it's called a practice for a reason. Be patient with yourself.

Journaling: Your Personal Time Machine

Writing about your experiences, thoughts, and emotions can be incredibly powerful. It's like having a conversation with yourself, one where you can be completely honest.

Maria, a 48-year-old marketing executive, discovered the power of journaling: "I started journaling as a way to vent. But over time, it became so much more. I could see patterns in my thoughts and behaviors. I could track my progress. And on tough days, I could look back and see how far I'd come."

Action Step: Start a journal. Don't worry about perfect prose. Just write. Try these prompts:

- How am I feeling today, and why?

- What's one thing I'm proud of myself for?

- If I could tell my estranged family member one thing without consequences, what would it be?

Writing Your Story: Becoming the Hero of Your Own Narrative

Here's a powerful exercise: Write your life story, focusing on the times you've faced challenges and come out the other side. This isn't about sugarcoating things. It's about recognizing your own strength and resilience.

Alex, a 55-year-old business owner, found this transformative: "When I wrote my story, I realized I'd been through tough times before and survived. I'd even thrived. It made me feel like I could handle this estrangement, too. I wasn't a victim; I was a survivor."

Action Step: Set aside some time to write your story. Focus on:

- challenges you've faced

- how you overcame them

- what you learned from each experience

- how these experiences have shaped who you are today

Creative Outlets: Expressing the Inexpressible

Sometimes, words aren't enough to express what we're feeling. That's where creative outlets come in. Whether it's painting, music, dance, or any other form of art, creativity can be a powerful healing tool.

Samantha, a 37-year-old graphic designer, found solace in art: "I started painting as a way to express emotions I couldn't put into words. The canvas became a safe space where I could pour out my anger, sadness, and hope. It was messy but so healing."

Action Step: Explore a creative outlet. Don't worry about being "good" at it. The goal is expression, not perfection.

Setting Boundaries: Your Emotional Forcefield

Learning to set and maintain healthy boundaries is crucial, especially when dealing with family estrangement. It's about protecting your well-being and creating space for healing.

Establishing Limits

Setting boundaries isn't about building walls. It's about creating healthy limits that protect your emotional well-being.

David, a 45-year-old engineer, learned the importance of boundaries: "I used to let my estranged sister's words cut deep. Every interaction left me drained. Learning to set boundaries - like limiting our conversations to certain topics or durations - was a game-changer. I could engage without being depleted."

Action Step: Identify areas in your life where you need stronger boundaries. It might be with your estranged family member or in other relationships. Write down specific boundaries you want to establish.

Communicating Clearly

Clear, assertive communication is key when setting boundaries. It's about expressing your needs and limits without aggression or apology.

Lisa, a 50-year-old teacher, shares her experience: "I had to learn to say no without feeling guilty, to express my needs without fear. It was uncomfortable at first, but it got easier with practice. And the respect I gained—from others and myself—was worth it."

Action Step: Practice assertive communication. Use "I" statements to express your needs and feelings. For example, "I need space when I'm feeling overwhelmed" instead of "You're always pressuring me."

The Art of Saying No

Learning to say no is a crucial part of setting boundaries. It's about recognizing your limits and honoring them.

James, a 42-year-old social worker, learned the power of no: "I was always a yes person, especially with family. Even after the estrangement, I'd bend over backward if my estranged brother asked for anything. Learning to say no was hard, but it was also freeing. It allowed me to prioritize my own well-being."

Action Step: Start small. Say no to a minor request that you'd usually agree to out of obligation. Notice how it feels. Remember, every time you say no to something that doesn't serve you, you're saying yes to your own well-being.

Forgiveness and Acceptance: Letting Go of the Weight

Forgiveness and acceptance are often misunderstood. They are not about excusing harmful behavior or pretending everything is okay. They are about freeing yourself from the burden of anger and resentment.

Self-Forgiveness: Being Your Own Best Friend

Self-forgiveness is about letting go of self-blame and guilt. It's recognizing that you're human, and humans make mistakes.

Mike, a 60-year-old retiree, found peace through self-forgiveness: "I spent years blaming myself for the estrangement with my son. If only I'd been a better father; if only I'd said this or done that. Learning to forgive myself was the hardest but most important step in my healing."

Action Step: Write a letter of forgiveness to yourself. Acknowledge your pain and perceived mistakes and offer yourself compassion and forgiveness.

Taming Your Inner Critic

We all have that inner voice that can be our harshest critic. Learning to recognize and reframe that voice is key to self-compassion.

Emily, a 42-year-old lawyer, learned to tame her inner critic: "My inner voice was brutal. It constantly reminded me of my failings as a daughter. I started to challenge that voice. When it said, 'You're a terrible daughter,' I'd counter with, 'I'm doing the best I can with the tools I have.' It didn't silence the critic entirely, but it balanced things out."

Action Step: Pay attention to your self-talk. When you notice negative self-talk, pause. Ask yourself: Would I say this to a friend? If not, how can I rephrase it more compassionately?

Forgiving Others: Releasing the Burden

Forgiving others doesn't mean you have to reconcile or that you're okay with what happened. It's about releasing the hold that person or situation has on you.

James, a 55-year-old professor, found freedom in forgiveness: "Forgiving my parents was something I did for me, not for them. It didn't erase the past, but it freed me from being constantly angry. It allowed me to move forward."

Action Step: If you're ready, consider writing a letter of forgiveness to the person you're estranged from. You don't have to send it. The act of writing itself can be cathartic.

Acceptance: Embracing Reality

Acceptance is about acknowledging reality as it is, not as you wish it to be. It's a powerful step toward peace.

Sarah, a 48-year-old nurse, found peace through acceptance: "For years, I fought against the reality of my estrangement from my brother. I kept thinking, 'This isn't how it's supposed to be.' Accepting that this was our current reality—not liking it, but accepting it—was liberating. It allowed me to focus on building my life rather than fighting against reality."

Action Step: Practice mindful acceptance. When you find yourself resisting reality, take a deep breath and say, "This is how things are right now. I may not like it, but I can accept it and work from here."

Redefining Identity: Becoming Who You Were Meant to Be

Family estrangement often forces us to question our identity. Who are we outside of our family roles? This is an opportunity to redefine yourself on your own terms.

Personal Growth: Turning Pain Into Power

Use your experience as a catalyst for growth. What can you learn from this? How can it make you stronger?

Alex, a 40-year-old entrepreneur, used his pain as fuel: "The estrangement from my parents was painful, but it pushed me to really figure out who I am and what I want. I started my own business, something I might not have had the courage to do if I was still trying to live up to their expectations."

Action Step: Set personal growth goals. What skills do you want to develop? What aspects of yourself do you want to strengthen?

New Narratives: Rewriting Your Story

Create a new narrative about yourself that isn't defined by the estrangement. Focus on your strengths, achievements, and positive qualities.

Lena, a 38-year-old writer, reshaped her narrative: "I used to introduce myself as 'the black sheep' of my family. Now, I see myself as resilient, creative, and compassionate. The estrangement is part of my story, but it doesn't define me."

Action Step: Write a new bio for yourself. Focus on your strengths, values, and aspirations. Who are you becoming?

Exploring New Roles and Identities

Family estrangement often leaves us feeling unmoored from our familiar roles. This can be an opportunity to explore new aspects of your identity.

Carlos, a 45-year-old teacher, found new purpose: "After the estrangement from my parents, I felt lost. I'd always been 'the good son.' Without that role, who was I? I started volunteering at a local community center and discovered a passion for mentoring youth. Now, I see myself as a community leader and mentor. It's a role that feels more authentic to who I am."

Action Step: Try on new roles. Volunteer, join a club, or take a class on something you've always been curious about. Pay attention to what feels energizing and authentic to you.

Building Resilience: Bouncing Back Stronger

Resilience isn't about never falling down. It's about getting back up every time.

Learning and Development: Feeding Your Mind

Engage in activities that promote learning and personal development. This could be taking courses, attending workshops, or simply reading widely.

Tom, a 50-year-old accountant, found strength in learning: "I started taking online courses in psychology. Understanding family dynamics and human behavior helped me make sense of my own situation. Plus, learning something new gave me a sense of progress and achievement."

Action Step: Choose a topic you're interested in and commit to learning more about it. It could be directly related to your situation (like family psychology) or something completely different.

Volunteering and Helping Others: Finding Purpose in Service

Giving back to others can provide a sense of purpose and fulfillment. It reminds us that we have value to offer the world.

Maria, a 45-year-old teacher, found healing through volunteering: "I started volunteering at a local youth center. Helping kids who were struggling with family issues gave me perspective on my own situation. It also reminded me that I have something valuable to offer, regardless of my family status."

Action Step: Look for volunteer opportunities in your community. Choose a cause that resonates with you.

Developing a Growth Mindset

A growth mindset—the belief that you can develop your abilities through dedication and hard work—can be a powerful tool in building resilience.

Jake, a 39-year-old software developer, embraced a growth mindset: "I used to think my personality was fixed. The estrangement happened, and I thought, 'This is just who I am now—damaged goods.' But everything shifted when I started to see every challenge as an opportunity to grow. Even the pain of estrangement became a chance to develop emotional strength."

Action Step: When you face a challenge, ask yourself, "What can I learn from this?" Focus on the process and effort, not just the outcome.

Planning for the Future: Creating Your Own Path

While healing from the past is important, looking forward is equally crucial. Planning for the future can give you a sense of control and hope.

Setting Goals: Charting Your Course

Set both short-term and long-term goals. These give you direction and a sense of purpose.

David, a 35-year-old graphic designer, found motivation in goal-setting: "After the estrangement, I felt lost. Setting goals—from small ones like 'cook a new recipe this week' to big ones like 'start my own design firm'—gave me something to focus on beyond the pain."

Action Step: Set three goals—one for this week, one for this year, and one for the next five years. Make them specific and achievable.

Visioning a Positive Future: Dreaming Big

Allow yourself to imagine a positive future, free from the constraints of past estrangement. This vision can inspire hope and resilience.

Emma, a 42-year-old HR manager, found power in visioning: "I created a vision board of what I wanted my life to look like in five years. It had nothing to do with my estranged family. It was all about my dreams—travel, career success, close friendships. It reminded me that I have a future to look forward to, regardless of my family situation."

Action Step: Create a vision board or write a detailed description of your ideal life five years from now. Let yourself dream big.

Creating New Traditions

Part of moving forward is creating new traditions that reflect your values and aspirations.

Sophia, a 50-year-old entrepreneur, found joy in new traditions: "Holidays were always tough after the estrangement. So, I decided to create my own traditions. Now, every Thanksgiving, I host a

'Friendsgiving' for others who might be alone. It's become something I look forward to all year."

Action Step: Think about times of the year that are difficult due to estrangement. How can you create new, meaningful traditions for these times?

Embracing Imperfection: The Beauty of Being Human

As we work on ourselves, it's easy to fall into the trap of perfectionism. But healing isn't about becoming perfect; it's about embracing our full, messy, beautiful humanity.

The Power of Vulnerability

Brené Brown, a researcher known for her work on vulnerability, reminds us that vulnerability is not weakness; it's our most accurate measure of courage (Brown, 2018).

Alex, a 47-year-old teacher, learned to embrace vulnerability: "For years, I put up a tough front. I didn't want anyone to know how much the estrangement hurt me. But when I finally opened up to a friend, it was like a weight lifted. Being vulnerable allowed me to connect more deeply with others and with myself."

Action Step: Share something you've been keeping to yourself with a trusted friend. It doesn't have to be about the estrangement—just practice the act of opening up.

Celebrating Small Wins

In the journey of healing, it's essential to acknowledge and celebrate your progress, no matter how small it might seem.

Liam, a 36-year-old accountant, found power in celebrating small wins: "I used to only focus on the big picture—was I over the estrangement yet? But when I started to celebrate small things—like getting through a holiday without breaking down or setting a boundary with a friend—I felt more motivated and positive."

Action Step: At the end of each day, write down three small wins. They could be as simple as "I practiced self-compassion today" or "I reached out to a friend."

Wrapping Up: Your Healing Journey

Remember, healing from family estrangement is a deeply personal journey. There's no one-size-fits-all approach. Be patient with yourself, celebrate small victories, and, most importantly, be kind to yourself along the way.

You're doing the work, and that's what matters. Each step you take in self-compassion and personal growth is a step toward a more fulfilling life. You've got this, and you're not alone on this journey.

As we close this chapter, take a moment to acknowledge how far you've come. You're here, you're learning, you're growing. That's something to be proud of.

In the next chapter, we'll explore paths to possible reconciliation. But remember, whether reconciliation happens or not, the work you're doing here is invaluable. You're building a strong, resilient you—and that's a beautiful thing.

Your journey of healing and self-discovery is ongoing. There will be ups and downs, steps forward and steps back. That's okay. That's part of being human. What matters is that you're committed to your growth and well-being.

As you move forward, carry with you the tools and insights you've gained. Practice self-compassion daily. Nurture your support network.

Take care of your physical and emotional health. Set and maintain healthy boundaries. Work on forgiveness and acceptance - of yourself and others. Continue to redefine your identity and build your resilience.

Remember that you are not defined by your family estrangement. You are a whole, worthy person with unique gifts to offer the world. Your experiences, including the difficult ones, have shaped you, but they do not limit you. You have the power to write the next chapters of your life story.

Be proud of yourself for doing this work. It takes courage to look inward, to face difficult truths, and to commit to personal growth. You're doing it, and that's remarkable.

As you close this chapter and prepare for the next, take a deep breath. Feel the strength within you. You've come this far, and you have the resilience to keep going. Trust in your journey, trust in your growth, and above all, trust in yourself.

The Bullet Points

This chapter focuses on personal growth and healing strategies for individuals dealing with family estrangement. It emphasizes the importance of self-care, building resilience, and redefining identity. Use this summary as a guide to your healing journey and as a reminder of the key concepts and practices introduced in this chapter.

- **Self-Compassion**
    - Treat yourself with kindness and understanding.
    - There are three components: self-kindness, common humanity, and mindfulness.
    - Take a self-compassion break during stressful moments.
- **Building Support Systems**

- o   Cultivate relationships with chosen family and friends.
- o   Seek mentors and role models who've experienced estrangement.
- o   Engage with supportive communities.

- **Comprehensive Self-Care**
  - o   Physical health: Get regular exercise and proper nutrition.
  - o   Sleep hygiene: Establish consistent sleep routines.
  - o   Mindfulness and meditation: Practice daily for emotional regulation.
  - o   Journaling: Express thoughts and track progress.
  - o   Creative outlets: Use art, music, etc., for emotional expression.

- **Setting Boundaries**
  - o   Establish and communicate personal limits.
  - o   Practice assertive communication.
  - o   Learn to say no without guilt.

- **Forgiveness and Acceptance**
  - o   Practice self-forgiveness and tame your inner critic.
  - o   Consider forgiving others as a way to release emotional burdens.
  - o   Work on accepting reality as it is, not as you wish it to be.

- **Redefining Identity**
  - o   Use the experience as a catalyst for personal growth.

- o   Create new narratives about yourself.
- o   Explore new roles and identities beyond family roles.

- **Building Resilience**
  - o   Engage in continuous learning and personal development.
  - o   Consider volunteering to find purpose in service.
  - o   Develop a growth mindset.

- **Planning for the Future**
  - o   Set short-term and long-term goals.
  - o   Create a vision for a positive future.
  - o   Establish new personal traditions.

- **Embracing Imperfection**
  - o   Recognize the power of vulnerability.
  - o   Celebrate small wins in your healing journey.

- **Ongoing Journey**
  - o   Acknowledge that healing is a process with ups and downs.
  - o   Continually practice self-compassion and personal growth.
  - o   Remember that you are not defined by family estrangement.

Remember: Your journey of healing and self-discovery is ongoing. Be patient with yourself, celebrate your progress, and trust in your ability to create a fulfilling life, with or without reconciliation. You have the power to write the next chapters of your life story.

Part 3:

The Road to Reconciliation

As we enter Part 3 of our journey through family estrangement, we face perhaps the most challenging and hopeful phase: the potential for reconciliation. This section explores the complex process of rebuilding relationships while also acknowledging that sometimes, moving forward means finding peace without reconciliation. These chapters offer guidance, strategies, and support for navigating this intricate terrain.

Chapter 5 focuses on the process of reaching out to your estranged adult child. We'll explore the delicate balance of timing, approach, and communication necessary when attempting to bridge the gap of estrangement. This chapter provides practical advice on crafting initial outreach, setting realistic expectations, and managing your own emotions throughout this sensitive process. You'll find guidance on respecting boundaries, practicing patience, and maintaining hope, even when the path to reconciliation seems uncertain.

Chapter 6 confronts a difficult reality: What if reconciliation doesn't happen? This chapter offers compassionate strategies for finding peace and purpose when the relationship remains strained or severed. We'll explore ways to redefine your sense of self and family, nurture other meaningful relationships, and channel your energy into personal growth and community involvement. This chapter reminds us that a fulfilling life is possible, even in the face of ongoing estrangement.

Chapter 7 addresses the ongoing journey of healing and growth, whether reconciliation occurs or not. Here, we'll discuss strategies for maintaining progress, dealing with setbacks, and continuing to evolve in your understanding of yourself and your relationships. This chapter emphasizes the importance of ongoing self-care, the value of support systems, and the power of resilience in navigating the long-term impacts of estrangement.

Throughout these chapters, you'll encounter real-life stories from individuals at various stages of the reconciliation journey. Some have successfully rebuilt relationships, others have found peace without reconciliation, and some are still navigating the complexities of strained family dynamics. These diverse experiences offer valuable insights and remind us that there's no one-size-fits-all approach to healing from estrangement.

As you engage with this section, remember that the road to reconciliation—or to peace without it—is rarely straight or simple. It's a path that requires courage, patience, and an ongoing commitment to personal growth. Whether you're taking tentative steps toward rebuilding a relationship or learning to thrive independently, this section offers tools and perspectives to support your journey.

It's crucial to approach this phase with self-compassion and realistic expectations. Healing from estrangement is a process, not a destination. There may be steps forward and steps back. Celebrate your progress, no matter how small, and be gentle with yourself during challenging times.

Remember that the goal of this journey isn't just about the outcome of your estranged relationship. It's about your personal growth, ability to find peace and fulfillment, and capacity to live authentically, regardless of external circumstances. Whether reconciliation becomes a reality or remains a hope, the work you do here will contribute to your overall well-being and resilience.

Chapter 5:

Reaching Out With Heart and Hope

You've done some heavy lifting in the previous chapters. You've worked on understanding yourself, healing your wounds, and building your resilience. Now, you're considering taking that next big step: reaching out to your estranged adult child. This chapter is all about helping you navigate that journey with compassion, wisdom, and hope.

But before we dive in, let's take a deep breath together. This process isn't about perfection; it's about progress, patience, and perseverance. Remember, you're not alone in this. Many parents have walked this path before you, and many are walking it alongside you right now.

Reflecting on Your Own Resilience

Before you reach out, it's crucial to check in with yourself. Are you emotionally ready for this step? Let's explore what that might look like.

Signs of Emotional Readiness

Sarah, a 55-year-old teacher, shares her experience: "I knew I was ready to reach out when I could think about the estrangement without feeling overwhelmed by anger or despair. I still felt sad, but it was a calm sadness. I realized I was strong enough to handle whatever response I might get."

Some signs that you might be ready include:

- You can think about the estrangement without being consumed by intense emotions.

- You've done work on yourself and understand your role in the conflict.

- You're open to hearing your child's perspective, even if it's difficult.

- You're prepared for the possibility that reconciliation might not happen immediately or at all.

Reviewing Your Personal Growth

Take a moment to reflect on how far you've come. What changes have you made? How have you grown?

Mark, a 60-year-old businessman, reflects: "Before reaching out, I made a list of all the ways I'd changed since the estrangement. I'd been to support groups, read books on communication, and even took an anger management course. Seeing that list gave me confidence that I was in a better place to rebuild our relationship."

Action Step: Write down three significant ways you've grown or changed since the estrangement. How might these changes positively impact your relationship with your child?

Understanding Your Intentions

Be clear about why you want to reconcile. Is it for your child's benefit, your own, or both?

Lisa, a 50-year-old nurse, shares: "I had to be honest with myself. At first, I wanted to reconcile because I missed my daughter, and it hurt to be estranged. But I realized that wasn't enough. I needed to want what was best for her, even if that meant continued separation."

Reflect on these questions:

- What are your hopes for reconciliation?

- Are you prepared to respect your child's wishes, even if they differ from yours?

- Can you approach reconciliation with an open heart and mind?

Choosing the Right Time

Timing can be crucial when reaching out. It's about finding a balance between taking action and respecting your child's space.

Assessing the Timing

Consider both your readiness and what you know about your child's current life circumstances.

John, a 58-year-old accountant, recalls: "I was tempted to reach out right before my daughter's wedding. But I realized that could put unnecessary pressure on her during an already stressful time. I waited until a few months after, which turned out to be much better timing."

Factors to consider:

- Are there any significant events or stressors in your child's life right now?

- Is there a meaningful date coming up that might provide a natural opening?

- Have you given enough time for emotions to settle since the last interaction?

The Virtue of Patience

Remember, reconciliation is a process, not an event. Rushing it can do more harm than good.

Maria, a 62-year-old retiree, advises: "I wanted to fix things immediately. But I realized my son needed time. I had to learn to be patient, to let him set the pace. It was hard, but it showed him I respected his boundaries."

Practice patience by:

- reminding yourself that healing takes time

- focusing on your own growth while waiting for the right moment

- finding healthy ways to manage your anxiety about reaching out

Setting a Positive Tone

When you do reach out, create an environment conducive to positive communication.

Tom, a 56-year-old teacher, shares: "I made sure I was in a calm state of mind before I wrote my letter. I chose a quiet Sunday morning, went for a walk first, and really centered myself. I wanted my peace and love to come through in my words."

Tips for setting a positive tone:

- Choose a time when you're feeling calm and centered.

- Ensure you have privacy and won't be interrupted.

- Consider the timing from your child's perspective; avoid high-stress periods in their life.

Crafting Your Message

How you reach out can be as important as when you do it. Let's explore how to craft a message that opens the door to reconciliation.

Choosing Your Method

Consider what method of communication might be most comfortable for your child.

Emma, a 53-year-old designer, explains her choice: "I knew my son preferred writing to talking, especially about emotional topics. So, I decided to write him a letter. It gave him space to process my words without feeling put on the spot."

Options to consider:

- **Letter or Email:** Allows for thoughtful composition and gives the recipient time to process
- **Phone Call:** More personal, but can be more emotionally charged
- **In-Person Meeting:** Most intimate but also potentially most intense

Writing With Empathy

Put yourself in your child's shoes as you compose your message.

David, a 59-year-old engineer, shares his approach: "I tried to imagine how my daughter might feel reading my words. I focused on acknowledging her feelings and experiences rather than just explaining my own."

Tips for empathetic writing:

- Use "I" statements to express your feelings without blaming.
- Acknowledge their perspective and feelings.
- Express regret for any hurt you've caused without expectation.

Key Elements to Include

A well-crafted message often includes several important components.

Sarah, a 57-year-old librarian, describes her letter: "I started by acknowledging the pain of our estrangement. Then, I apologized for my role in it. I expressed my love for my son and my hope for reconciliation, but I also made it clear that I would respect his wishes."

Consider including:

- an acknowledgment of the estrangement and its impact
- a sincere apology for your role in the conflict
- an expression of love and care for your child
- a clear statement of your hope for reconciliation
- respect for their feelings and decisions

Respecting Boundaries

Respecting boundaries is crucial in rebuilding trust and creating a healthy relationship.

Understanding Their Boundaries

Recognize that your child may need different levels of contact or intimacy than you do.

Mark, a 61-year-old retiree, learned this lesson: "I wanted to jump right back into weekly dinners and daily calls. But my daughter needed to start with just occasional texts. It was hard, but respecting her boundaries showed her I was committed to changing our dynamic."

Tips for respecting boundaries:

- Pay attention to verbal and non-verbal cues about comfort levels.
- Ask directly about their preferences for communication.
- Be willing to start with less contact than you might prefer.

Setting Your Own Boundaries

It's also important to establish your own healthy boundaries in the reconciliation process.

Lisa, a 54-year-old teacher, shares: "I had to learn that reconciliation didn't mean I had to tolerate disrespect. I set clear boundaries about how I expected to be treated, which actually helped rebuild mutual respect."

Consider:

- What behaviors are you comfortable with?
- What are your deal-breakers?
- How can you communicate your boundaries respectfully?

Balancing Persistence and Patience

Finding the right balance between reaching out and giving space can be tricky.

John, a 59-year-old businessman, reflects: "I had to learn when to reach out and when to step back. I'd send a message, then wait for a response without pushing. It showed my son I was there but not forcing things."

Guidelines for balance:

- Reach out periodically, but don't bombard them with messages.

- If they don't respond, wait before trying again.

- Respect their need for space, even if it's more than you'd like.

Effective Communication Strategies

Once you've made initial contact, how you communicate can make or break the reconciliation process.

Active Listening

Really hearing your child's perspective is crucial for rebuilding trust.

Emma, a 56-year-old nurse, shares her experience: "I had to learn to truly listen, not just wait for my turn to speak. When I repeated back what I heard my daughter saying, it showed her I was really trying to understand."

Tips for active listening:

- Give your full attention when they're speaking.

- Reflect back what you've heard to ensure understanding.

- Ask open-ended questions to encourage them to share more.

Non-Defensive Language

Avoiding defensiveness can help keep conversations productive.

Tom, a 63-year-old retiree, learned this lesson: "When my son brought up past hurts, my first instinct was to defend myself. But I learned to say, 'I understand that hurt you' instead of 'But I didn't mean to.' It made a huge difference in our conversations."

Strategies for non-defensive communication:

- Acknowledge their feelings without trying to change them.

- Use "I" statements to express your own feelings.

- Avoid "but" statements, which can negate what came before.

Expressing Genuine Emotions

Authentic emotional expression can help rebuild connection.

Sarah, a 58-year-old artist, shares: "I learned to be vulnerable with my son. Instead of just saying 'I'm fine,' I'd share when I was feeling sad or scared. It helped him see me as a real person, not just 'Mom.'"

Tips for expressing emotions:

- Name your feelings specifically (e.g., "I feel sad" rather than "I feel bad").

- Share the thoughts or situations that lead to these feelings.

- Express emotions without expecting a specific response.

Apologizing Sincerely

A heartfelt apology can be a powerful step toward healing.

Crafting a Genuine Apology

A meaningful apology acknowledges the hurt caused and takes responsibility.

Mark, a 60-year-old teacher, describes his approach: "I didn't just say, 'I'm sorry if you were hurt.' I said, 'I'm sorry that my actions hurt you.' I acknowledged specific things I'd done wrong and how they impacted my daughter."

Elements of a sincere apology:

- clear acknowledgment of the hurtful action
- taking full responsibility without making excuses
- expressing genuine remorse
- committing to do better in the future

Addressing Specific Incidents

Being specific in your apology shows that you've really reflected on past events.

Lisa, a 55-year-old accountant, shares: "I made a list of specific incidents I needed to apologize for. It was hard, but addressing each one showed my son I was serious about making amends."

Tips for addressing specific incidents:

- Be concrete about what happened.

- Acknowledge the impact of your actions.

- Avoid justifying or explaining away your behavior.

Avoiding Justifications

Resist the urge to explain or justify your past actions in your apology.

John, a 62-year-old retiree, learned this lesson: "I wanted to explain why I'd acted the way I did. But I realized that could sound like I was making excuses. Instead, I focused on acknowledging the hurt I'd caused, without any 'buts.'"

Remember:

- An apology is about the other person's hurt, not your intentions.

- Explanations can often sound like excuses.

- It's okay to offer explanations later if they ask, but keep the apology clean.

Offering to Rebuild the Relationship

After the initial reconnection, it's time to think about how to move forward.

Suggesting Next Steps

Propose ways to rebuild your relationship, but be open to their ideas.

Emma, a 59-year-old librarian, shares her approach: "I suggested we start with monthly coffee dates. But I also asked my daughter what she thought would work best. Showing I was willing to follow her lead helped her feel more comfortable."

Ideas for next steps:

- regular check-ins (calls, texts, or emails)
- scheduled in-person meetings
- shared activities or hobbies

Being Open to Their Terms

Be willing to rebuild the relationship on your child's terms, even if they differ from your ideal.

Tom, a 64-year-old engineer, learned flexibility: "I wanted to jump back into our old weekly dinners. But my son wanted to start with just texting. It wasn't what I hoped for, but I realized meeting him where he was comfortable was more important than getting what I wanted."

Remember:

- Their comfort level may be different from yours.
- Be willing to start smaller or slower than you might prefer.
- Show appreciation for any steps they're willing to take.

Setting Realistic Expectations

Understand that rebuilding trust and closeness takes time.

Sarah, a 57-year-old teacher, shares her realization: "I had to accept that we couldn't go back to how things were before the estrangement overnight. Setting realistic expectations helped me appreciate small progress instead of feeling disappointed."

Tips for managing expectations:

- Recognize that reconciliation is a process, not an event.
- Celebrate small steps forward.
- Be prepared for setbacks and view them as part of the process.

Handling Their Response

Preparing for various possible responses can help you navigate this sensitive time.

Preparing for Different Outcomes

Your child's response might range from enthusiastic to hesitant to negative.

Mark, a 61-year-old businessman, shares his experience: "I tried to prepare myself for any response. My daughter's initial reaction was cautious, which was hard. But because I'd mentally prepared, I was able to respect her need for time."

Possible responses to prepare for:

- enthusiasm and readiness to reconnect
- caution and need for time
- anger or hurt that needs to be expressed
- no response at all

Managing Your Emotions

How you handle your own emotions can greatly impact the reconciliation process.

Lisa, a 56-year-old nurse, reflects: "When my son didn't respond to my first letter, I was devastated. But I had a support system in place to help me process those feelings without pushing him."

Strategies for emotional management:

- Have a support system ready (friends, therapist, support group).

- Practice self-care and stress-reduction techniques.

- Remind yourself that their response isn't a reflection of your worth.

Being Patient

Give your child time and space to process and respond in their own way.

John, a 63-year-old retiree, learned patience: "I wanted an immediate response, but my daughter needed weeks to process my letter. Giving her that time, without pressuring her, showed I respected her needs."

Remember:

- Everyone processes emotions and makes decisions at their own pace.

- Pushing for a quick response can backfire.

- Use this time to focus on your own growth and healing.

Maintaining Open Communication

If your initial outreach is well-received, focus on keeping lines of communication open.

Checking in Regularly

Consistent, respectful communication can help rebuild your relationship.

Emma, a 58-year-old designer, shares her approach: "We started with weekly texts. Just a 'How are you doing?' or sharing a memory. It was a small thing, but it helped rebuild our connection."

Ideas for check-ins:

- regular texts or emails

- scheduled phone calls

- sharing photos or articles of mutual interest

Encouraging Honest Dialogue

Create a safe space for open, honest communication.

Tom, a 62-year-old teacher, learned the importance of openness: "I made it clear to my daughter that I wanted to hear her truth, even if it was hard for me to hear. It wasn't always easy, but it built trust between us."

Tips for encouraging honesty:

- Respond calmly to difficult truths.

- Express appreciation for their openness.

- Be willing to be vulnerable yourself.

Showing Consistent Effort

Demonstrate your commitment through consistent actions over time.

Sarah, a 59-year-old accountant, shares: "I made sure to follow through on every promise, no matter how small. If I said I'd call, I called. It showed my son he could trust my words."

Ways to show consistent effort:

- Follow through on commitments.
- Remember important dates and events.
- Show interest in their life and experiences.

Seeking Professional Support if Needed

Sometimes, professional help can provide valuable guidance in the reconciliation process.

Recognizing When to Seek Help

Be open to the idea that professional support might benefit your reconciliation efforts.

Mark, a 60-year-old retiree, found value in therapy: "When we hit a roadblock in our communication, I suggested family therapy. It gave us tools to work through our issues that we wouldn't have found on our own."

Signs professional help might be beneficial:

- Communication keeps breaking down despite your best efforts.
- Old patterns of conflict keep resurfacing.
- You're struggling to manage your own emotions in the process.

Exploring Family Therapy

Family therapy can provide a neutral space to work through issues together.

Lisa, a 57-year-old teacher, shares her experience: "Family therapy was challenging but so helpful. Having a neutral third party helped us see patterns we couldn't see on our own."

Benefits of family therapy:

- neutral ground to discuss difficult topics
- professional guidance in communication strategies
- tools for resolving conflicts and setting boundaries
- a structured environment for healing and growth

For those who don't have easy access to a therapist, consider joining support groups or online forums to learn more about strategies for working with your family.

Utilizing Support Groups

Connecting with others who are on similar journeys can provide comfort and practical advice.

John, a 64-year-old retired teacher, found solace in a support group: "Joining a support group for estranged parents was eye-opening. I learned I wasn't alone, and I got practical tips from others who had been through similar situations."

Benefits of support groups:

- shared experiences and understanding
- practical advice from those who've been there
- a sense of community and belonging
- opportunity to both give and receive support

Remember, seeking help isn't a sign of weakness. It's a sign of commitment to healing and growth.

Conclusion: The Journey of Reconciliation

Let's take a moment to reflect on the journey ahead. Reconciliation is not a destination, but an ongoing process. It requires patience, perseverance, and a whole lot of love.

Recap of Key Points

Let's revisit some of the crucial steps we've discussed:

1. Reflect on your own resilience and readiness.
2. Choose the right time to reach out.
3. Craft a thoughtful, empathetic message.
4. Respect boundaries—both theirs and yours.
5. Use effective communication strategies.

6. Apologize sincerely and specifically.

7. Offer to rebuild the relationship on their terms.

8. Be prepared for various responses.

9. Maintain open, consistent communication.

10. Seek professional help if needed.

Words of Encouragement

Emma, a 61-year-old who successfully reconciled with her daughter after five years of estrangement, offers these words of hope: "There were times I thought we'd never speak again. The journey was hard, with many setbacks. But every small step forward was worth it. Today, we have a relationship that's different from before, but in many ways, it's stronger and more authentic. Don't give up hope."

Remember:

- Every small step matters.

- Healing takes time.

- You're showing immense courage by taking this journey.

Final Thoughts: Love, Patience, and Perseverance

The road to reconciliation is rarely smooth or straight. It requires love—not just for your child but for yourself. It demands patience—with the process, with your child, and with yourself. And it calls for perseverance—the willingness to keep trying, even when it's difficult.

Tom, a 65-year-old who reconciled with his son after seven years of estrangement, shares: "There were times I wanted to give up. But I kept reminding myself why this was important. I held onto love, even when it was hard. I practiced patience, even when it felt endless. And I persevered, even when it seemed hopeless. In the end, it was all worth it."

As you get started on this journey, remember:

- Your efforts matter, regardless of the outcome.

- You're growing and healing through this process.

- You're not alone—many others are on similar journeys.

Real-Life Stories of Successful Reconciliation

Let's close this chapter with a few stories of families who have successfully navigated the path to reconciliation. While every situation is unique, these stories can offer hope and inspiration for your own journey.

Sarah and Mike's Story: The Power of a Sincere Apology

Sarah, 58, and her son Mike, 32, were estranged for three years following a heated argument about Mike's career choices. Sarah shares their reconciliation story:

"I realized I had been trying to control Mike's life instead of supporting his choices. I wrote him a letter, taking full responsibility for my actions and apologizing sincerely. I told him I loved him and respected his decisions, even if they were different from what I had envisioned.

"Mike didn't respond immediately, which was hard. But a month later, he called. We started with short, slightly awkward phone calls, which gradually became longer and more open. It took time, but we rebuilt our relationship. Today, we're closer than ever, and I've learned to appreciate Mike for who he is, not who I thought he should be."

Key Takeaway: A genuine apology that takes responsibility without making excuses can open the door to healing.

The Johnson Family: Healing Through Family Therapy

Mark (62) and Lisa (60) Johnson were estranged from their daughter Amy (35) for four years. The whole family shares their reconciliation journey:

Mark: "We had a lot of unresolved issues that led to the estrangement. When Amy agreed to try family therapy, it was a turning point."

Lisa: "The therapist helped us see patterns we were blind to. We learned to communicate without blame and to really listen to each other."

Amy: "Therapy gave us a safe space to express our feelings. It wasn't easy, but it allowed us to understand each other better."

Mark: "We had to confront some hard truths about ourselves and our parenting. But it led to genuine change and healing."

Today, the Johnsons have a renewed relationship based on mutual respect and understanding.

Key Takeaway: Professional help can provide valuable tools and insights for navigating complex family dynamics.

David and Emily: The Journey of Small Steps

David, 59, reconciled with his daughter Emily, 28, after six years of estrangement. They share their story of gradual reconnection:

David: "I reached out with a letter, apologizing and expressing my love for Emily. She responded cautiously, agreeing to email communication."

Emily: "I wasn't ready for face-to-face meetings, but emails felt safe. We started with short messages, sharing small parts of our lives."

David: "I had to learn patience. Sometimes Emily wouldn't respond for weeks, but I respected her pace."

Emily: "Over time, as I saw Dad's consistent effort and respect for my boundaries, I felt more comfortable. We progressed to texts, then phone calls."

David: "It took almost two years before we met in person. But that first hug was worth every moment of waiting."

Today, David and Emily enjoy a close relationship built on a foundation of mutual respect and understanding.

Key Takeaway: Respecting boundaries and being willing to take small, consistent steps can lead to meaningful reconciliation over time.

Appendices

Sample Initial Outreach Letter

Dear [Child's Name],

I hope this letter finds you well. I've been thinking about you a lot, and I wanted to reach out. I know our relationship has been difficult, and we've been estranged for some time now. I want you to know that I love you, and I miss having you in my life.

I've spent a lot of time reflecting on our past, and I realize that I've made mistakes that have hurt you. I want to take full responsibility for my actions and sincerely apologize for [specific actions or behaviors]. I understand now how my behavior impacted you, and I'm truly sorry.

I've been working on myself, trying to understand our dynamics better and improve my communication skills. I hope we might have the opportunity to rebuild our relationship, but I want you to know that I respect your feelings and your boundaries.

If you're open to it, I'd love to hear from you. We could start small—maybe with emails or texts if that feels comfortable. But please know that I'll respect whatever decision you make.

No matter what, I want you to know that I love you, I'm proud of you, and I'm here if you ever want to connect.

With love and hope, [Your Name]

Resource List

Books:

- *Reconciling with Estranged Adult Children* by Tina Gilbertson
- *I Only Say This Because I Love You* by Deborah Tannen
- *Adult Children of Emotionally Immature Parents* by Lindsay C. Gibson

Support Groups:

- Estranged Parents of Adult Children Support Group (online)
- Parents of Estranged Adult Children Meetup Groups (various locations)

Websites:

- www.estrangedstories.com
- www.reconnectionclub.com

Reflective Exercises

- **Letter to Your Younger Self:** Write a letter to yourself at the time when the estrangement began. What advice would you give? What insights have you gained?

- **Gratitude Journal:** Each day, write down three things you're grateful for about your child or your journey of growth.

- **Emotion Mapping:** Create a "map" of your emotions throughout the reconciliation process. This can help you recognize patterns and triggers.

Remember, the journey to reconciliation is unique for every family. These tools and stories are meant to guide and inspire, not to prescribe a one-size-fits-all solution. Trust your instincts, be patient with the process, and above all, lead with love and respect—both for your child and for yourself.

As you move forward, hold onto hope but also embrace the growth and healing you're experiencing, regardless of the outcome. Your efforts to heal, understand, and connect are valuable in themselves. You're doing important, courageous work. Be proud of every step you take on this journey.

The Bullet Points

This chapter provides guidance on how to approach reconciliation with estranged adult children. It covers preparing yourself emotionally, crafting your outreach and communication strategies, and navigating the reconciliation process. Use this summary as a reference guide for your reconciliation journey.

Key Points

- **Reflecting on Your Own Resilience**
    - Assess emotional readiness for reconciliation.
    - Review personal growth since estrangement.
    - Understand your intentions for reconciling.

- **Choosing the Right Time**
    - Consider timing in relation to your child's life circumstances.
    - Practice patience in the reconciliation process.
    - Set a positive tone for communication.

- **Crafting Your Message**
    - Choose an appropriate method of communication (letter, email, phone, in-person).
    - Write with empathy, acknowledging your child's perspective.
    - Include key elements: acknowledgment, apology, expression of love, and respect for their feelings.

- **Respecting Boundaries**
    - Understand and respect your child's boundaries.
    - Set your own healthy boundaries.
    - Balance persistence with patience in reaching out.

- **Using Effective Communication Strategies**

- Practice active listening.
- Use non-defensive language.
- Express genuine emotions.
- Apologize sincerely and specifically.

- **Offering to Rebuild the Relationship**
  - Suggest next steps for reconnection.
  - Be open to rebuilding on your child's terms.
  - Set realistic expectations for the reconciliation process.

- **Handling Their Response**
  - Prepare for different possible outcomes.
  - Manage your own emotions throughout the process.
  - Be patient and give your child time to respond.

- **Maintaining Open Communication**
  - Establish regular check-ins if initial outreach is well-received.
  - Encourage honest dialogue.
  - Show consistent effort in maintaining contact.

- **Seeking Professional Support**
  - Recognize when professional help might be beneficial.
  - Consider family therapy as an option.
  - Utilize support groups for estranged parents.

Remember: Reconciliation is an ongoing process that requires patience, perseverance, and love. Every small step matters, and your efforts contribute to your own growth and healing, regardless of the outcome.

Chapter 6:

How to Move on Without Reconciliation

Life doesn't always unfold the way we hope or plan. Sometimes, despite our best efforts and deepest desires, reconciliation with our estranged adult child doesn't happen. This chapter is for those of you facing this difficult reality. It's about finding peace, purpose, and even joy in your life, even when the relationship you long for remains out of reach.

The Power of Acceptance

Acceptance isn't about giving up or approving of the situation. It's about acknowledging reality as it is rather than as we wish it to be. This can be one of the most challenging yet liberating steps in your journey.

The Importance of Acceptance for Mental Health

Sarah, a 62-year-old retired teacher, shares her experience: "For years, I fought against the reality of my estrangement from my son. I was constantly stressed, anxious, and depressed. It wasn't until I started to accept the situation that I found some peace. It didn't change the facts, but it changed how I lived with them."

Acceptance can benefit your mental health in several ways:

- reduced stress and anxiety

- improved mood and emotional stability

- better sleep and physical health

- increased ability to focus on the present and future

Dr. Lisa Johnson, a psychologist specializing in family estrangement, explains: "Acceptance allows us to stop expending energy fighting against reality. This frees up mental and emotional resources for healing and personal growth."

Differentiating Between Giving Up and Moving On

It's crucial to understand that accepting the current reality of estrangement is not the same as giving up hope or stopping to care.

Mark, a 58-year-old accountant, reflects: "I struggled with the idea of acceptance because I thought it meant I was abandoning my daughter. My therapist helped me see that I could accept the current situation while still holding space for possible future reconciliation. It's not giving up; it's giving myself permission to live fully in the meantime."

Key differences between giving up and moving on:

- Giving up often comes from a place of despair; moving on comes from a place of self-care.

- Giving up closes the door entirely; moving on leaves the door open while building a life on your side of it.

- Giving up often involves bitterness; moving on involves working toward peace.

Stories of Finding Peace Without Reconciliation

Emily, 65, estranged from her daughter for 12 years: "I tried everything to reconcile with my daughter. Letters, therapy offers, even moving closer to her city. Nothing worked. It was devastating. But over time, I learned to find joy in other areas of my life. I deepened friendships, became involved in my community, and eventually found a sense of peace. I still love my daughter and hope for reconciliation, but I've learned that my happiness can't be dependent on it."

James, 70, estranged from his son for 20 years: "The hardest part was letting go of the future I had imagined—grandchildren, family holidays, all of it. But once I accepted that I couldn't control my son's choices, only my own, things began to shift. I focused on being the best person I could be and on living a life I could be proud of. It doesn't erase the pain, but it gives me purpose and contentment."

These stories remind us that while the pain of estrangement may never completely disappear, it's possible to build a meaningful, joyful life alongside it.

Continuing Self-Care and Personal Growth

Acceptance isn't a one-time event; it's an ongoing process. It's crucial to continue prioritizing self-care and personal growth.

Pursuing Outlets and Social Connections Through Hobbies and Interests

Engaging in activities you enjoy can provide a sense of purpose, accomplishment, and connection.

Linda, 59, found solace in gardening: "After my daughter cut contact, I felt lost. I started gardening as a way to nurture something. I joined a local gardening club and made new friends. Watching things grow and bloom reminded me that life goes on, and beauty can still be found."

Ideas for exploring hobbies and interests:

- Take a class on something you've always wanted to learn.

- Join a club related to your interests (book clubs, hiking groups, art classes).

- Volunteer for a cause you're passionate about.

- Start a creative project (writing, painting, crafting).

- Learn a new skill (cooking, language, instrument).

Making New Connections Through Support Groups

Support groups can provide understanding, validation, and a sense of community.

Tom, 63, shares: "Joining a support group for parents of estranged adult children was a turning point for me. For the first time, I didn't feel alone. We share our stories and our pain, but also our triumphs and strategies for moving forward. These people have become like family to me."

Benefits of support groups:

- shared experiences and understanding

- practical advice and coping strategies

- opportunity to help others, which can be healing in itself

- reduced feelings of isolation and shame

Continuing Daily Journaling and Personal Growth

Maintaining a practice of self-reflection and personal development can help you continue to heal and grow.

Maria, 61, found power in journaling: "I've kept a journal throughout this journey. It's been a place to vent my feelings, track my progress, and set intentions for my future. Looking back at earlier entries, I can see how far I've come. It reminds me that healing is possible, even if it's slow."

Ideas for personal growth practices:

- daily gratitude journaling
- setting and working toward personal goals
- reading self-help or inspirational books
- practicing mindfulness or meditation
- engaging in regular physical exercise

Remember, investing in your own growth and well-being is not selfish. It's necessary for your healing and can positively impact all areas of your life.

Redefining Family Relationships

One of the challenges of estrangement is reimagining what family means to you. This can be painful, but it can also open doors to new, fulfilling relationships.

Building a Chosen Family

The concept of "chosen family"—close relationships with people who may not be blood relatives—can be particularly meaningful for those experiencing estrangement.

David, 68, shares his experience: "After years of estrangement from my son, I realized I was isolating myself. I started reaching out to old friends and making new ones. Over time, these friends became my family. We celebrate holidays together and support each other through hard times. It doesn't replace my son, but it fills my life with love and belonging."

Ways to build a chosen family:

- Deepen existing friendships.

- Be open to forming new connections, regardless of age or background.

- Participate in regular group activities or traditions.

- Be the kind of friend you want to have—supportive, reliable, and caring.

Strengthening Other Personal Relationships

While dealing with estrangement, it's easy to overlook other important relationships in your life. Nurturing these can provide support and fulfillment.

Lisa, 57, found renewed connection with her sister: "I was so focused on my estranged daughter that I had neglected my relationship with my sister. As I worked on accepting the estrangement, I also worked on rebuilding that sisterly bond. It's become one of the most important relationships in my life."

Relationships to consider nurturing:

- siblings

- extended family members

- long-time friends

- spouse or partner

Remember, strengthening these relationships isn't about replacing your estranged child. It's about creating a supportive network and recognizing the love that is present in your life.

Community Involvement and Volunteering

Engaging with your community and giving back can provide a sense of purpose and connection, turning your painful experience into a force for good.

Finding Purpose Through Helping Others

Many people find that helping others provides a sense of meaning and perspective.

John, 66, found healing through volunteering: "I started volunteering at a youth mentoring program. Working with these kids, I realized I still had so much to offer. It didn't erase the pain of estrangement from my own son, but it gave me a way to channel my paternal instincts positively. Knowing I'm making a difference in these young lives brings me joy and purpose."

Ideas for community involvement:

- Mentor young people.

- Volunteer at local charities or community organizations.

- Participate in community events or local government.

- Offer your professional skills to non-profit organizations.

- Join or start a community improvement project.

Turning Your Experience Into a Positive Force

Your journey through estrangement has given you unique insights and empathy. You can use these to help others facing similar challenges.

Margaret, 70, turned her pain into purpose: "After years of working through my own estrangement, I started a support group in my community for other parents of estranged adult children. Helping others navigate this journey has been incredibly fulfilling. It's given meaning to my experience and allowed me to create something positive out of my pain."

Ways to help others through your experience:

- Share your story (in support groups, through writing, or public speaking).

- Offer to be a listening ear for others going through estrangement.

- Advocate for more awareness and support for family estrangement issues.

- Create resources (like blogs or podcasts) to support others.

Remember, your experience, though painful, has given you valuable wisdom. Sharing that wisdom can be healing for both you and others.

More Real Life Stories: Moving on Without Reconciliation

Let's look at some more inspiring stories of individuals who have found ways to move forward and find fulfillment, even without reconciliation.

Emily's Story: Finding New Purpose

Emily, 64, has been estranged from her daughter for 15 years:

"The first few years were the hardest. I felt like I was in a fog of grief. But slowly, I started to rebuild my life. I joined a hiking club and discovered a passion for nature photography. These new friends became my support system.

"I also started volunteering at a women's shelter. Helping women rebuild their lives gave me a sense of purpose. It didn't fill the hole left by my daughter, but it gave me a way to channel my maternal instincts positively.

"I still hope for reconciliation one day, but I've learned that I can't put my life on hold. I've created a life filled with meaning, friendship, and even joy. The pain of estrangement is still there, but it no longer defines me."

Robert's Journey: Redefining Family

Robert, 71, has been estranged from both his children for over two decades:

"Losing contact with my kids felt like losing a limb. I went through all the stages of grief—denial, anger, bargaining, depression. Acceptance was the hardest and took the longest.

"What helped me was redefining what family meant to me. I strengthened my relationship with my brother and became closer to my nieces and nephews. I also formed deep friendships with a group of men my age. We meet weekly, support each other through hard times, celebrate the good times. They've become my chosen family.

"I've also found joy in unexpected places. I took up painting and discovered I had a talent for it. My art has become a way to express my emotions and connect with others.

"The void left by my children will always be there, but I've built a life around it that's rich and fulfilling. I'm at peace with who I am and the life I've created."

Sarah's Path: Turning Pain into Purpose

Sarah, 68, has been estranged from her son for 18 years:

"For years, I defined myself by my estrangement. I was the mother whose son didn't want her. It was a heavy identity to carry.

"The turning point came when I joined a support group for estranged parents. Hearing others' stories made me realize I wasn't alone. It also made me want to help.

"I trained as a counselor specializing in family estrangement. Now, I help others navigate this painful journey. It's given purpose to my pain. Every person I help feels like a small victory against the pain of estrangement.

"I've also learned to find joy in the present. I travel, I've taken up ballroom dancing, I nurture my friendships. My life isn't what I imagined it would be, but it's rich and meaningful in its own way.

"The door is always open for my son if he chooses to reconnect. But I've learned that my happiness can't depend on that. I've found peace in living my life fully, here and now."

"These stories remind us that while the pain of estrangement may always be present, it's possible to build a life of meaning, purpose, and even joy alongside it. Moving forward doesn't mean forgetting or stopping to care. It means choosing to live fully despite the pain.

Strategies for Continued Healing

As you continue on this journey of moving forward without reconciliation, here are some strategies to support your ongoing healing:

- **Practice Self-Compassion:** Be kind to yourself. Recognize that you're doing the best you can in a difficult situation.

- **Set New Goals:** Having things to work towards can provide a sense of purpose and forward momentum.

- **Create New Traditions:** Especially around holidays or times that are particularly difficult.

- **Express Your Feelings:** Through art, writing, music, or any medium that resonates with you.

- **Stay Open to Joy:** Allow yourself to experience happiness without guilt.

- **Continue Therapy or Counseling:** Regular check-ins with a mental health professional can support your ongoing healing.

- **Practice Mindfulness:** Stay connected to the present moment rather than dwelling on the past or worrying about the future.

- **Maintain Boundaries:** If there is limited contact with your estranged child, ensure it's on terms that are healthy for you.

- **Keep the Door Open:** While moving forward with your life, you can still maintain an openness to reconciliation if circumstances change.

- **Share Your Wisdom:** Consider mentoring or supporting others who are earlier in their estrangement journey.

Embracing Your New Chapter

Moving forward without reconciliation doesn't mean you've failed or that you're giving up on your child. It means you're choosing to live your life fully despite the pain of estrangement. This takes tremendous courage and strength.

Remember, your relationship with your child does not determine your worth. You are a whole, valuable person with much to offer the world. The love you have for your child doesn't disappear because you're focusing on your own well-being.

As you embrace this new chapter, be proud of your resilience, celebrate your growth, and acknowledge the strength it takes to keep moving forward. Your journey may not be what you expected, but it can still be rich, meaningful, and filled with love.

You've weathered one of life's most challenging storms. In doing so, you've gained wisdom, empathy, and strength. These are gifts you can now share with the world.

As we close this chapter, remember that your story isn't over. This is just the beginning of a new chapter—one where you are the author, free to write a future filled with purpose, connection, and joy. Your journey continues, and it holds endless possibilities for growth, love, and fulfillment. Embrace it with an open heart and a spirit of hope.

You've got this, and you're not alone. Keep moving forward, one step at a time, towards the fulfilling life you deserve. Your journey of healing and self-discovery continues, and it's a beautiful thing to witness. Be kind to yourself, stay open to joy, and remember—your life is yours to live, and it can be wonderful in ways you might not yet imagine.

The Bullet Points

This chapter addresses the challenging reality of moving forward when reconciliation with an estranged adult child doesn't occur. It offers guidance on finding peace, purpose, and joy in life despite ongoing estrangement. Use this summary as a reference for strategies to heal and thrive.

- **The Power of Acceptance**
    - Understand acceptance versus giving up.
    - Know the benefits of acceptance for mental health.
    - Differentiate between moving on and abandoning hope.

- **Continuing Self-Care and Personal Growth**
    - Pursue hobbies and interests for social connections.
    - Join support groups for shared experiences.
    - Maintain daily journaling and personal development practices.

- **Redefining Family Relationships**
    - Build a chosen family of close friends.
    - Strengthen other personal relationships (siblings, extended family).
    - Find new ways to experience family connections.

- **Community Involvement and Volunteering**
    - Find purpose through helping others.
    - Turn personal experience into a positive force.

    - Engage in mentoring or community projects.
- **Real-Life Stories of Moving On**
    - Emily's story: Finding new purpose through nature and volunteering
    - Robert's journey: Redefining family and discovering new talents
    - Sarah's path: Turning pain into purpose by helping others
- **Strategies for Continued Healing**
    - Practice self-compassion.
    - Set new personal goals.
    - Create new traditions.
    - Express feelings through creative outlets.
    - Stay open to joy without guilt.
    - Continue therapy or counseling.
    - Practice mindfulness.
    - Maintain healthy boundaries.
    - Keep the door open for potential future reconciliation.
    - Share wisdom with others facing similar challenges.
- **Embracing Your New Chapter**
    - Recognize personal worth beyond the parent-child relationship.
    - Celebrate resilience and personal growth.

- View life as an ongoing journey of self-discovery.

Remember: Moving forward without reconciliation is not giving up on your child. It's choosing to live your life fully while still holding space for love. Your journey continues, and it holds possibilities for growth, connection, and fulfillment in ways you might not yet imagine.

Chapter 7:

Wrapping Up

As we reach the end of this journey together, I want to take a moment to acknowledge the courage and resilience you've shown in exploring these challenging topics. Whether you've found a path to reconciliation or are learning to move forward without it, your commitment to growth and healing is truly commendable.

Finding Peace in Your New Reality

Whatever the outcome has been for you, my deepest hope is that you've found a measure of peace and a new way of living that brings joy and happiness. Life after estrangement—whether reconciled or not—is about rediscovering yourself and creating a life that aligns with your values and brings you fulfillment.

Sarah, a 65-year-old retiree, shares her perspective: "After years of estrangement from my son, I realized that my happiness couldn't be dependent on reconciliation. I had to find joy in my life as it was. It wasn't easy, but as I focused on my passions and cultivated new relationships, I found a sense of peace I never thought possible."

Remember, finding peace doesn't mean you've stopped caring or that the pain has completely disappeared. It means you've learned to coexist with your experiences and emotions in a way that allows you to live a full and meaningful life.

The Power of Trusting in Life

Trusting in life is indeed critical to our emotional well-being. This trust isn't about believing everything will always go our way but about having faith in our ability to handle whatever life brings.

Mark, a 58-year-old teacher, reflects: "Learning to trust in life again was a turning point for me. After the estrangement, I was always waiting for the next bad thing to happen. But gradually, I realized that I had survived one of the most painful experiences of my life, and I was still standing. That gave me confidence to face whatever came next."

Trusting in life involves:

- accepting that we can't control everything
- believing in our resilience and ability to adapt
- focusing on what we can influence rather than what we can't
- finding meaning and purpose even in difficult circumstances
- embracing uncertainty as a natural part of life

Insights From Our Journey

As we conclude, let's revisit some key insights that can continue to guide you on your path forward:

Exploring Family Value Systems

Understanding our family's value system can provide profound insights into the roots of estrangement. These values, often passed down through generations, shape our beliefs, behaviors, and expectations.

Lisa, a family therapist, explains: "Many times, estrangement occurs when there's a significant clash in values between generations. Exploring these value systems can help us understand why certain conflicts arose and how they escalated to estrangement."

Take time to reflect on your family's values:

- What principles were emphasized in your upbringing?
- How have these values shaped your relationships?
- Are there values you've adopted or rejected as an adult?

Understanding these dynamics doesn't excuse hurtful behavior, but it can provide context and pave the way for greater empathy and understanding.

The Power of Empathy

Empathy—the ability to understand and share the feelings of another—is a powerful tool in healing relationships. It allows us to see the world through the eyes of our estranged loved ones, even when we disagree with their actions.

John, a 60-year-old father reconciling with his daughter, shares: "When I finally tried to see things from my daughter's perspective, it was like a light bulb went on. I didn't agree with all her choices, but I could understand why she felt hurt and angry. That understanding was the first step towards rebuilding our relationship."

Practicing empathy involves:

- listening without judgment
- trying to understand the other person's feelings and motivations
- acknowledging their perspective, even if you don't agree

- recognizing that their feelings are valid, even if their actions are hurtful

Remember, empathy doesn't mean excusing harmful behavior. It's about understanding, which can lead to more constructive communication and healing.

Breaking the Cycle of Blame and Resentment

One of the most crucial steps in healing from estrangement is breaking the cycle of blame and resentment. This cycle can keep us trapped in pain and prevent us from moving forward.

Dr. Emma Thompson, a psychologist specializing in family dynamics, explains: "Blame and resentment are like poison. They hurt us more than the person we're angry with. Letting go of these feelings doesn't mean we're excusing harmful behavior. It means we're choosing to free ourselves from the burden of carrying that anger."

Steps to break the cycle:

1. Acknowledge your feelings of hurt and anger.
2. Take responsibility for your part in the conflict.
3. Practice forgiveness—of yourself and others.
4. Focus on what you can control in the present.
5. Choose to let go of resentment as an act of self-care.

The Impact of Early Attachment

Our early experiences of attachment in childhood play a significant role in shaping our adult relationships. Secure attachment in childhood is often linked to healthier relationships in adulthood.

Dr. James Carter, a child psychologist, explains: "The patterns of attachment we form in our early years create a template for our future relationships. Secure attachment provides a foundation of trust and emotional security that can help us navigate conflicts more effectively in adulthood."

Understanding your attachment style can provide valuable insights:

- How did your early relationships shape your expectations in adult relationships?

- Are there patterns in your relationships that might stem from your attachment style?

- How can you work towards developing more secure attachments in your current relationships?

While we can't change our past, understanding these patterns can help us make conscious choices to create healthier relationships in the present.

The Role of Self-Reflection and Understanding Family Dynamics

Self-reflection and a deep understanding of family dynamics are powerful tools that can lead either to reconciliation or to a healthy acceptance of estrangement.

Maria, a 55-year-old mother who reconciled with her son after years of estrangement, shares: "It wasn't until I really looked at myself and our family patterns that things started to change. I had to confront some hard truths about my parenting and our family dynamics. It was painful, but it led to real change and eventually reconciliation."

On the other hand, Tom, a 62-year-old father who has accepted his estrangement, reflects: "Understanding our family dynamics helped me see why reconciliation might not be possible right now. It's sad, but this understanding has allowed me to find peace and live my life fully while still leaving the door open for the future."

Self-reflection and understanding family dynamics involve:

- examining your own behaviors and patterns
- looking at intergenerational patterns in your family
- understanding how family roles and expectations have shaped relationships
- recognizing dysfunctional patterns that may have contributed to estrangement

Whether this understanding leads to reconciliation or acceptance of estrangement, it's a crucial step in your healing journey.

Your Ongoing Journey

As we conclude this book, remember that your journey doesn't end here. Healing, growth, and self-discovery are lifelong processes. There may be setbacks along the way, but each challenge is an opportunity for further growth and understanding.

Here are some final thoughts to carry with you:

- **Be Kind to Yourself:** You're navigating one of life's most challenging experiences. Treat yourself with the same compassion you'd offer a dear friend.
- **Stay Open to Growth:** Continue to learn, reflect, and evolve. Every experience, even painful ones, can lead to greater wisdom and strength.
- **Nurture Your Connections:** Whether it's with family, friends, or a chosen family, cultivate relationships that bring positivity and support to your life.

- **Find Meaning in Your Experiences:** Consider how you can use your journey to help others or contribute positively to the world.

- **Hold Onto Hope, but Don't Let It Hold You Back:** While it's okay to hope for reconciliation, ensure that this hope doesn't prevent you from living fully in the present.

- **Trust in Your Resilience:** You've survived one of life's most challenging experiences. Trust in your ability to handle whatever comes next.

- **Embrace Joy Without Guilt:** Allow yourself to experience happiness and fulfillment, regardless of the status of your estranged relationship.

Remember that your worth is not defined by any single relationship. You are a whole, valuable person with much to offer the world. The love you have for your estranged family member doesn't disappear because you're focusing on your own well-being.

As you move forward, be proud of your journey. Celebrate your growth. Acknowledge the strength it takes to keep moving forward, trust in life, and open your heart to new possibilities.

Your story is still unfolding, and it holds endless potential for love, growth, and fulfillment. Embrace it with an open heart and a spirit of hope. You've weathered one of life's most challenging storms, and in doing so, you've gained wisdom, empathy, and strength. These are gifts you can now share with the world.

As we part ways, know that you carry with you the tools, insights, and strength to continue your journey of healing and growth. Trust in yourself, trust in the process of life, and remain open to the beautiful possibilities that each new day brings.

Your journey continues, and it is a beautiful, courageous thing to witness. May you find peace, joy, and fulfillment as you write the next chapters of your life story. Remember, you are the author of your life, and you have the power to create a future filled with love, meaning, and happiness.

Thank you for allowing me to be a part of your journey. May your path forward be filled with healing, growth, and moments of joy. You've got this, and you're not alone. Here's to your continued journey of self-discovery and the beautiful life that awaits you.

References

Blake, L. (2015). *Hidden voices: Family estrangement in adulthood*. Standalone. https://www.standalone.org.uk/wp-content/uploads/2015/12/HiddenVoices.FinalReport.pdf

Brown, B. (2018). *Dare to Lead*. Random House.

Neff, K. (2024). *What is self-compassion?* Self-Compassion. https://self-compassion.org/what-is-self-compassion/

Pillemer, K. (2022). *Fault lines*. Penguin.

Salleh, M. R. (2018). Life event, stress and illness. *The Malaysian Journal of Medical Sciences: MJMS*, *15*(4), 9–18. https://www.ncbi.nlm.nih.gov/pmc/articles/PMC3341916/

Made in the USA
Monee, IL
27 December 2024